I WAS A SLAVE IN RUSSIA

I WAS
A SLAVE
IN
RUSSIA

AN AMERICAN TELLS HIS STORY

By John Noble

THE DEVIN-ADAIR COMPANY · NEW YORK · 1958

Canadian agent: Thomas Nelson & Sons, Ltd., Toronto

Library of Congress catalog card number: 57-13354

Designed by Lewis F. White

Printed in the United States of America

I WAS A SLAVE
IN RUSSIA

IT IS HARD TO DE-scribe a nightmare adequately, unless you can say how the day had been before the night fell. The worst time may come after a good calm day, when the night turns into a horror.

For me, it came out of days that were filled with new hopes and with dreams for the days to come. It came on a very good day, and it happened like this.

1 DRESDEN, CRUMBLED by the giant blows of American air raids, moved restlessly and expectantly in its ruins. It was the first week of May, 1945. War sounds of a new sort had been heard from east and west. On May 6, just sixty-five miles to the west, American soldiers were pushing against the last lines of German resistance. To the east, Russian troops were moving toward the city.

For my family, in our house high above Dresden on Bergbahn Strasse (the Street of the Mountain Railway), the sounds meant something far different from what they meant to any of our neighbors.

Throughout the war we had been locally interned by Hitler's forces. We were not permitted to leave the city, and every third day we had to register with the police. We were under constant observation by the Gestapo. Yet we were treated well, even courteously.

For we were enemy aliens, American citizens. I was born in the United States. My father and mother, born in Germany, and my brother, born in Switzerland, were naturalized Americans and remain so to this day. The war sounds of May 6, therefore, meant that our countrymen were coming—and peace. Peace, at long, weary last.

Perhaps, though, we were listening more closely to the

west than to the east, where the Soviet cannonading was.

Dresdeners knew that the war was really ending. The only question was which side would reach Dresden first, the east or the west. Many hoped it would be the east, the Russians; the horrors of American air raids were fresh in their minds.

There had been rumors of Russian outrages in other parts of the country, but these were only rumors. Few people believed them.

And so May 6 was cannon fire in the distance and anxiety on the streets. The night before had been sleepless in the Noble house. We all were up at dawn. We knew, as the whole town did, that today probably would see the gunfire and everything pretty well decided.

A pair of artillery glasses mounted on our sun porch gave a view of the entire city. As soon as it was light enough to see, we began turning the glasses slowly back and forth. There seemed to be no movement at all. Even stranger, we heard no sound. To my father, this all meant that the end of the race was near. The Americans, we hoped, would be the first in. Why not, suggested my father, raise the American flag? We had painstakingly made the flag from bits of cloth in anticipation of a day that we feared would never really come. The only times we ever had taken it from its hiding place were those times of fear and suspense when American planes rode high in the skies, and the siren howls sent the Germans scurrying for shelter. We would spread the flag out on the bright white tiles of the big terrace that extended from the house on all sides.

My father's proposal sent my brother George and me racing up to the roof, the flag in our arms. It was all very exciting; we didn't know what might happen as we stuck

4

our heads out. There might be shots from the silent town. Anything. We hesitated a moment, then were out on the roof, feet braced precariously on the slates. Hastily we fastened the flag to a rod and hung it out.

We ducked back in and waited. Still not a sound. Then we heard my father calling to us to come quickly. We ran down to the porch and looked out over the city. Miraculously, it seemed, from windows, from rooftops—from almost every building—white flags had begun to pop out. Within minutes the city below us was a field of white flags of every size and construction, flapping in the breeze or being waved frantically.

The appearance of our flag had been like the squeeze on a trigger, releasing the town's nervous pressure. The people had been poised and waiting for a conqueror—as we had been waiting for a liberator.

The town waited silently, behind its façade of white flags.

An hour later we knew who had won the race for Dresden. From our porch, through the artillery glasses, we saw a soldier. His uniform seemed to be made up of ragged odds and ends; but the shoulder boards, askew on his tunic, were what counted. They were red.

The occupying forces flooded in. The highway from Bautzen was lined for miles with the horse carts in which the Red army traveled through Germany. Drunken soldiers roistered along the road. The fighting was over, and there was no discipline. Permission had been given the soldiers to pillage and rape. Marshal Zhukov had issued the order: full liberty for the Red army to do as it pleased for three days. But the horror was to go on unendingly for three weeks.

On that first day in Dresden we saw soldiers pulling mat-

5

tresses out of houses, and we knew they would be put to one of two uses: for drunken sleep or for rape. Rape was the sport of the day, and it was not done in private. The soldiers didn't care about privacy; the screaming victims couldn't.

One might hurry down a residential street and hear screams also from houses which one might have visited socially the week before.

Red flags now replaced the white. Swastikas had been carefully unstitched, leaving only a red field on which greetings to the conquerors had been scrawled: "WE THANK THE RED ARMY FOR FREEDOM, WORK, AND BREAD."

Before I left the house to look at "liberated" Dresden, George and I had taken a precaution which to some might have looked foolish. We simply had hung on the gate a sign that read "U.S. PROPERTY." To the Russians it must have seemed potent. Not one unauthorized Red soldier set foot on the property, even though drunken soldiers later in the month set fire to the Loisenhof, Dresden's best restaurant, across the street from us. And routed 300 persons out of a bomb shelter nearby and raped every woman there, regardless of age or condition. But the sign on our gate seemed to throw a circle of exemption around our house. It was easy to infer that the friendship of Russia and the United States was the reason.

I was 21 then. Before my next birthday I was to learn a lot more about that friendship.

Soon the sanctuary of the Noble home was being talked about among the people we knew in Dresden. In less than 48 hours after the Red troops had entered the city, while rape and pillage were at their height, thirty of our closest friends took shelter with us. No. 12 Bergbahn, perched on the highest point of the hills around the city and flying the American flag, must have seemed a genuine outpost of the United States.

A British prisoner of war, released from a Stalag camp when the Russians came through the German lines, had shown up at our gate seeking shelter. We gave him food, a bicycle, and directions, and after he had rested he went off westward to the American lines.

On the third day of the occupation, we crossed the street to the garage in which our car had been stored throughout the war. We had had no gas ration and, in any event, as aliens we couldn't have gone very far. It was a large, two-tone Audi convertible, and to reach it we required the co-operation of the garage keeper. To prevent the Russians from making off with the 100-odd vehicles in his charge, he had cut the wires to the elevator that led to the underground garage. There was, he explained to the Russians, no other way to get there. If they could repair it, of course . . . None even tried. Actually, he had only to put two wires together.

George and I painted a fairly "official"-looking American flag on the back trunk of the car and affixed two small flags to fender stanchions. Our "U.S." car was then ready for a trip to the American lines, sixty-five miles away. Father took the trip, with my brother George, a British-born neighbor, and an American friend. They were not stopped once.

At Grimma, a little town just west of the demarcation line and southeast of Leipzig, they spoke to some American officers. The town mayor, one Major Clark, said: "We'll do all we can. You're in good hands now, but you'll have to wait till early 1946. Space will be available then for civilians, and you can get back to the States."

This was not exactly what we had expected, but then the two years we had originally intended to stay in Europe had already been tripled, and a few more months wouldn't matter, we thought.

Our house continued immune to the abuses that the Russians were visiting upon the rest of the town, and even our camera factory had not been placed on the Russians' list of factories to be immediately dismantled and hauled to Russia. Father's "nothing-can-happen-to-us" attitude affected us and everything we did. We were secure in our house high on the hill.

Within the first few days of the occupation we tried to get the factory back into regular operation. George handled production details and I worked to straighten out the administrative end. Some changes had taken place, not all of them welcome. One worker who had been assigned to the factory as a functionary of the Nazi Arbeitsfront, the party's labor-union front, showed up with a Communist brassard proudly flaunted in place of his swastika armband. My father protested against some of the demands of the Nazi-turned-Communist and even took his complaint to the city officials. But there too he found that the Communist officials, by and large, were simply Nazi officials with new armbands.

May 13 brought new problems to our "America Island." Eight Americans, former prisoners of the Nazis, arrived. One, carried on a dapple-gray horse, was in a dying condition. We placed him on a stretcher and carried him to the Lahmans sanitarium, now run by the Russians.

As we stepped into the reception room, we saw vodka bottles in place of medicines, Russian drunks instead of flowers. The scent of vodka and stale tobacco smoke filled the place. We were greeted by a burly soldier who shouted, "Get out! This place is for Red army soldiers."

We carried the moaning soldier back to the house. Our family doctor came to examine him and gave him medicine to relieve the pain. That evening, half a dozen of our transient American guests left for the American lines, promising to send an ambulance when they arrived.

We waited, and while we waited the Russians set fire to the Loisenhof restaurant. They roared with laughter as the flames started to devour the building, but cursed and threatened us as, with the aid of our American visitors, we put out the fire.

That evening, more than twenty-four hours after the previous group had left for the west, the rest of the Americans also departed, all but the sick one; they in turn promised to send an ambulance. To our joy, an ambulance pulled up a few hours later; it had come at the request of the first contingent. The crew loaded the patient aboard and were off.

The second group, we later learned, also reached the American lines in safety and reported what was taking place in our section of Dresden. On the morning of May 15, half a dozen staff cars of the 76th Division drove up. Khaki cars had never looked more beautiful. Two officers came in to speak with us. Their principal mission, they said, was to find as many American soldiers as they could. We assured them of our help and offered to take them to the City Hall, where they might explain their purpose to the officials there.

The Russians, however, were quick to point out that they were not interested in rounding up American soldiers released from Nazi camps. It was none of our business either, they said, making it unmistakably clear that they had no intention of cooperating with the Nobles or with any other Americans, military or civilian.

The American officers, quietly furious and expecting no help from the Red army, settled upon making the Noble house a kind of official halfway station for returning soldiers. We spent the rest of the day cruising around the city with them in search of Americans. By nightfall we had returned home with thirty in tow.

It was arranged that cars of the 76th Division should come twice weekly to pick up soldiers from our house. But as it developed, they came twice a day, and always we had American soldiers to send back with them.

Things were working out. Our factory was in limited but healthy production. City Hall seemed to have accepted the fact that our house was a liaison station for messages and soldiers destined for the American zone. At one point, a Red officer came to the door, checked our papers, pronounced them in order, and offered to post guards if we felt the need. We gratefully declined, for the sign "U.S. PROPERTY" was working well. The Red army gave our factory an order for cameras, and there seemed not a cloud on the horizon.

Perhaps we had not been looking closely enough at the streets of Dresden. In the press of our own plans it was easy to ignore day-to-day occurrences—civilians stepping hastily off the sidewalks when Red soldiers approached; the continual drunkenness and rapings; the arrests. These disorders were all too easy to overlook as a part of the general disorder in the world. Tomorrow it would be all right again. There was always tomorrow.

In East Germany all optical plants had been dismantled and shipped to the Soviet Union. We had the problem, then, of obtaining lenses so that we could fill our Red army orders for cameras. When we explained this to the Dresden City Hall, we received permission from that source and from Red army headquarters to go west and see what might be done with American or West German help.

On June 28 my father and I left at seven in the morning on a trip to the American zone. We were to see a lens maker in Jena about making lenses for our factory. At eleven we reached the border. There was an argument with a Red guard about our papers, but finally we convinced him that they were in order, and we went on our way.

We had very poor success at Jena, because many officials of the German optical companies, Zeiss in particular, had already headed deeper into the western zone ahead of rumors that American forces might soon quit all Thuringia. We left an order for lenses, nevertheless, and went to Kassel, where American headquarters had been established. We planned to work out details there for setting up a plant in the American zone.

At Kassel we were assured there was no need to transplant our factory, or a part of it, to a western area, or to set up a new one there, since Dresden lay in a territory that sooner or later would come under British occupation.

Our trip back was a quiet one, and we felt a great surge of relief. When a British border guard who stopped us at his check point asked us half seriously if we wanted to commit suicide by returning to the Soviet zone, my father laughed.

It was late in the afternoon of July 5 that we crossed into the Soviet zone. The barbed-wire entanglements, the floodlights, the machine-gun nests that marked the border were soon behind us. Rain began to fall, and we nearly

11

had our only mishap, skidding and almost hitting a bridge abutment.

We reached Dresden shortly before midnight and drove directly to our house. We had seen one or two Russian guards patrolling the street, but they showed little interest in us. All was quiet, and there were no other people about, for none were permitted out of doors after nine.

We stopped at our gate, unpacked our things quickly, and rang the bell. George came out of the house and walked down rapidly to meet us. A civilian followed him. My father asked, "George, who is he?"

"Father, something is wrong." George's voice was tired and tight. Turning to the civilian and then back to us, he said, "They're putting you under arrest."

I glanced at the roof. The American flag was not there.

The days of security and complacency had ended.

The nightmare had begun. And it was to rule us for nine years.

2   LIGHTS BURNED IN OUR house all night, as we readied ourselves for what might follow. Mother explained what had happened in our absence. The Russian soldiers had come a few hours after we had left on our trip west. Six house guests, who had been driven from their own homes by fear of the liberators, were arrested and taken away for questioning. A number of American soldiers who had come from the American zone were also removed; they were held for five days, we learned later. Finally, every camera in the house was confiscated.

At no time, while they were being questioned, had George or my mother heard mention of a charge.

My father, still optimistic, was sure it was a misunderstanding. All would be straightened out in a day or two. But I noticed that the light shone in his room through the night.

At seven the following morning my father and I were taken, as prisoners of the Soviet political police, to NKVD headquarters in Dresden. We felt a moment of hope as we parked: two American jeeps stood by the building. Might the Americans be there to arrange our freedom? We were soon to find that they too were under arrest.

We were held at NKVD headquarters for three days. We were not formally questioned, but the officers conversed with us and sought obliquely the names of any relatives we might have in Germany. Still no charges were brought, no explanations offered for our arrest.

After the third day the headquarters was moved, and we were taken along, like so much furniture. At the new address, Bautzner Strasse 114, we were assigned to rooms in the attic. From my window I could look up the Elbe valley and see the glossy white brick tower of our house, the tower from which we had flown our flag.

At our new address, my only chance to speak to my father was on trips to the bathroom. On one trip he told me that an NKVD colonel had interviewed him. "You are no American citizen," he told my father. My father laughed this off as a clumsy intimidation. Then the colonel waved a sheet of paper under my father's face; it was a telegram, he said, a telegram from New York "proving" that my father was not a citizen. When my father replied that if a telegram in regard to his citizenship were sent at all, it could only prove his citizenship, and that it could only come from Washington, not from New York, the colonel stalked angrily from the room. Indeed, the attempt to frighten us was so clumsy that my father's attitude that the arrest was a mistake became more reasonable than ever.

Our food was drab, to say the least. We had noodles and canned meat, noodles and milk, noodles and fat or potatoes. It was a boring enough diet. Yet it was the best, bar none, that I was to eat for the better part of a decade.

On the evening of the twentieth the bill of fare was varied. One of the guards, in a state of excitement, brought us sandwiches. He also brought the news we had been waiting for: we were to be released. The sandwiches seemed almost a gesture of apology.

The next day we were all ready. I was called down to one of the NKVD offices, presumably for my leave-taking. A Captain Pankov was waiting for me. He looked and acted like NKVD officers: he took short, tight steps, his head slightly bowed, eyes turned up and peering from under frowning brows. It was the NKVD attitude and motion of continuous tension.

Captain Pankov seemed friendly. He greeted me with a smile, then got down to business, which I assumed would be a final routine questioning, the last go-around before the release.

"How much money have you?" he asked.

I took out my wallet, opened it, and went through my money. A 1000-mark note and 1860 marks in smaller denominations were there. I handed him the wallet, automatically palming the 1000-mark note. The next moment, I was glad I had done this.

14

"Take off your watch, please," Pankov said.

I handed it to him, and he wrote out a receipt for it and pushed it across the desk to me.

"Let me have your papers," he said.

He took these and made a little pile of them. My passport was there, my driver's license, birth certificate, and my papers from the Swiss consulate. The consulate had been in technical charge of enemy aliens in Germany during the war.

On top of the pile he plunked my silver cigarette case. (I don't smoke, but I always carried cigarettes to offer to others.)

"You will be taken to prison," he announced routinely. He must have seen my face tighten in alarm, for he explained the situation in his casual way: "You are to be called as a witness in your father's trial and then you will go free."

When I protested that my father, as an American citizen, hardly seemed liable to a Soviet trial proceeding, Pankov waved me away with a smile and said, "Our government knows exactly what it can and cannot do. That will be all."

A guard took me to a waiting car; my father was there before me. We had a whispered consultation as to the meaning of it all, and of one thing my father was sure. "Everything will turn out all right," he said.

The drive was a short one, down the hill and into the central part of Dresden. We headed into the partly bombed-out but still quite usable Münchenerplatz prison.

From the car we were taken inside; gate after gate clanged shut behind us, and the clanging echoed through the dark corridors. We were taken into a small office where a guard, in broken German, gave us instructions.

"Take off your belt and take the shoestrings from your shoes," he ordered. I had heard that this was standard procedure to prevent people from committing suicide, but only in the case of real criminals. Criminals! The thought whirled around in my mind. Criminals.

An escort took us to the second floor. I was led to cell number 5, my father in another direction. I walked into the cell and the guard slammed the iron door. The noise reverberated in my mind and through me. Alone, and with the noise of that great iron door filling the cell, all the feeling of dread that my father's optimism had kept away came over me in a wave. I was afraid and alone. The door had closed me in. And it had shut the world out.

In the door was a spy hole, and over the door a barred transom. Through the hole I could see my father being shoved through a door almost directly opposite. I stood for half an hour at the hole, staring at the faceless rows of doors. I wondered how many eyes were similarly peering through spy holes.

Then I heard the screams.

Someone was being whipped. The screams were clear but directionless, as though filtered through the thick walls of the prison. Later I was able to place the direction from which they came; the whippings took place in the "questioning room," in a wing of the building. It was at the opposite side of the prison from my cell and adjacent to one of Dresden's residential streets.

Suddenly a closer sound of violence slammed into the cell block. It came from the fourth floor. By looking sharply upward from the bottom edge of the spy hole I could see the hallway that ran past the fourth-floor cells. As I looked, a cell door opened. Guards dragged a struggling prisoner out and threw him to the floor. He tried

MÜNCHENERPLATZ PRISON

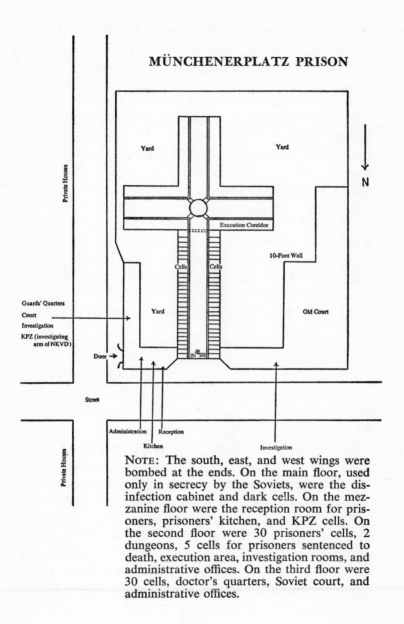

NOTE: The south, east, and west wings were bombed at the ends. On the main floor, used only in secrecy by the Soviets, were the disinfection cabinet and dark cells. On the mezzanine floor were the reception room for prisoners, prisoners' kitchen, and KPZ cells. On the second floor were 30 prisoners' cells, 2 dungeons, 5 cells for prisoners sentenced to death, execution area, investigation rooms, and administrative offices. On the third floor were 30 cells, doctor's quarters, Soviet court, and administrative offices.

to fight his way up, and they pounced on him and pinned him to the floor with their knees. Then they stripped him, tearing his shirt away and pulling his trousers off in a violent tug that left the prisoner tumbled head down in a heap against the wall.

One guard had a short leather whip. The other hastily pulled off his belt. Then they began beating the man, not slowly and methodically but rapidly and in semifrenzy. They kicked him and shoved him along the floor while they tore his skin with their cutting lengths of leather. His screams were terror-filled and anguished.

I couldn't keep from watching; the horror of it was hypnotic. Long after the guards had finished, panting, and had flung the bloody, whimpering man back into the cell, the scene and the sounds stayed on in my mind, even into sleep.

And added to them were new screams from the questioning room.

3 IT WAS SEVERAL DAYS before I realized the most important fact of prison life. This paramount concern, riding the days and nights like a monkey perched on the head, is food, the belly-craving that fills one like a cancer and crowds out everything else. On the first morning, it was the scenes and sounds of violence that preoccupied. Screams could be heard almost constantly from the questioning room. I learned, though, that the mind can erect barriers against such sounds, so that unless one tries one cannot hear them. Prisoners who couldn't shut them out didn't last long. They went mad. I was told that one of the many prisoners who attempted suicide tried to kill himself in his madness by crashing his head against the wall of his cell.

When food was first brought in to me, I still hadn't learned about the domination of the stomach when men are made to live like animals. The meal was a bowl of coffee-colored soup with a fishy taste. I threw it out without a second thought.

The day went easily and without incident. The cell was swarming with bugs, and I occupied myself by catching them and flipping them into the toilet bowl. At noon and in the evening, watery, fishy soup was again distributed, and again I poured it out. I told myself I didn't need it.

Within a very few days I realized how mistaken I was. Inexplicably, the food stopped coming. It didn't stop just for me; it stopped throughout the prison. There was no food for anyone. There was no explanation from the guards. "There will be food tomorrow," they said. There wasn't. Warm water with a coffee taste was passed out instead. Later in the day, the guards brought twenty-quart buckets from which they served, as solemnly as if it were food, plain warm water, yellowish and without taste.

Slowly, the stomach took over body and mind. There was no food the next morning, only more of the warm water. I had never really been hungry before. During our entire internment in Germany we had had the same food as everyone else in Dresden. Even the worst air raids had not deprived us altogether. The Germans never had cracked down on rations.

But now I began to know about hunger, and it was frightening. It was not just an emptiness; it was a positive, driving force, urgent and constantly on the mind—like the urgency of a schoolboy's body as he dreams his first pulsing dreams of sex.

I had to face the situation. I was alone in my cell, with no one to talk to, no one to turn to for help, except God, perhaps. Would He hear a prayer from me? Would He persuade those creatures in the prison corridors to open the door and bring me food, or even freedom? I spoke my prayers, asking God in heaven to comfort my body and soul.

I am sure many others in those prison walls were asking divine help too. And many outside the walls, for even the "free" people of Germany had had to pull in their belts a notch or two. Food was scarce. Everywhere, the Soviet troops had been trampling down stock rooms, looting. The stock room in Münchenerplatz prison had been full when the Russians arrived, but they had nearly emptied it, so that they might trade food for vodka or schnapps. Other food reserves had been carried away by the soldiers to feed the women they were using day and night. I found out later that, at the time we were starving in our cells, the guard and officers in my house were forcing my mother to cook our food for the girls whom the Russians brought into the house.

Three days passed and no food was distributed to us. At last, on the fourth day—which was July 31, 1945—a few ounces of bread and some thin soup were handed to me; on the fifth day, more of the same, but as I lay down that evening I had no idea that on the following morning would begin a twelve-day starvation period.

When it became apparent on the first of those days that there was to be no food, loud protests, uncontrolled curses and screaming were let loose. They became louder as the

20

second, third, and fourth days went by. Men went out of their minds, woman prisoners became hysterical. Some Moslem prisoners chanted their prayers.

Then death struck, right and left. Cell doors were opened and dead bodies pulled out by an arm or a leg. I wondered when it would be my father's turn and mine. When I no longer was strong enough to lift my feet off the floor, I put myself into the hands of God.

Some seven hundred prisoners had entered that starvation period. I was one of twenty-two or twenty-three that survived, along with my father.

Each day, as the guards brought the warm water around, they roused the prisoners with a cry of "breakfast" or "coffee." If the cry was "breakfast," there would be a tense silence as the prisoners waited to see if food was meant, or more water. And during those twelve days it was always the water.

On the thirteenth day my cell door opened and a guard, as indifferent as if he had been supervising a delivery of water, stepped into the cell. From a large container he took a tiny mound of bread crumbs wrapped in a piece of crumpled paper. The crumbs weighed two ounces.

I stared at the crumbs for twenty minutes, then ate them one at a time. They did little for the aching emptiness, but their dry, tasteless texture started the saliva flowing, and each crumb was an almost unbearable pleasure.

At noon, the usual buckets were brought to the cells. It was again warm water, mainly, that was ladled out, but also it had the aroma of soup. And the bottom of the bucket could not be seen through the liquid. It was that thick.

With bread and soup on the menu again, at least some of the prisoners who had survived the twelve days of starvation began to feel normal again. They could be seen standing and moving in their cells. Others were dying, however, from the lasting effects of hunger. As new prisoners were brought in, it was very evident that the "old-timers" had built a mental refuge for themselves. Compared to the horrors of the twelve days, to have a couple of cups of weak broth and a piece of bread meant a good life.

My cell was eight paces long and about six wide. It had one bed—a metal frame with fiber-stuffed pads for mattress. It folded back against the wall when not in use. Against one wall was a seatless toilet bowl, flushed from outside, and in a corner stood a short-handled broom, with which a prisoner was supposed to sweep the cell once a day.

Other men were brought in now to share my cell. I was pretty lucky in my companions, and never suffered from the overcrowding that was beginning to blight the existence of other prisoners. Some cells, of the same size as mine, had twenty occupants.

My first cell mates were a Russian-born doctor and a German farm boy. At night, we placed the mats on the floor and slept there, reserving the bed for a daytime seat.

Like virtually everyone else in the prison with whom I came in contact, they knew of no reason for being jailed. They did not know when, if ever, they would be released, or even sentenced. This ignorance of our fate was our prison sickness, far more curdling to the mind than a sentence to death or to a long term in prison would have been.

The third man sent to my cell was a forestry student. While I had almost wept with happiness to have the doctor and the farm lad share the world of my cell, it was the forestry student who did one of the greatest services possible. For reasons as mysterious as those for which he had been imprisoned in the first place, he was released. Before he left, I asked him if he could take a message to my house, so that my mother might know the whereabouts of my father and myself. Despite the peril of going near a house as suspect as was ours, he did deliver the message.

The word he carried meant fresh hope, of course, for the family. We were well. We certainly would be released, they reasoned. The power of the United States would turn the keys and open the doors. It was just a matter of time.

In prison, of course, one's hopes did not travel so far. It was enough that the word of our existence could be leaked out. There was no talk of release, or of the future from any aspect. I found that it did not take long to start thinking like a prisoner.

The conception of time disappeared from my mind, and I could think only as far as this: by God's grace I would live or die. Beyond that there was no planning, no dreaming, no hoping. The rotation of the earth from day to night, from season to season, held little meaning. Time was not measured by the clock. It progressed by pains, by screams, by weariness, by hunger.

4 A STRANGE FEAR RODE the entire population of East Germany, regardless of age, sex, occupation, or belief. The fear diminished in those who were imprisoned by the MVD (the NKVD were renamed MVD about this time), but it struck them again with full force when they were released. They had supposed that their prison experience would have hardened them against fear, but this was not so. To these prisoners, let loose in East Germany, where the Soviet terror is present on every street, release brought no joy beyond the momentary joy of seeing loved ones again.

Every ring of the doorbell, every knock on the door, every MVD car passing by brought the fear—the fear of being arrested again. When they were arrested again, they actually were relieved to be in prison once more. It meant, in a twisted, sick way, security for them. At least they knew. They didn't have to die inside any more when the doorbell sounded. The cell was sure and certain; they knew more or less what they could count on. Now all they had to worry about were the times the cell door opened to bring some change in their prison routine. It seemed that this sort of uncertainty, within the rigidity of the prison routine and the locked-in vault of the prison cell, was better than living in the "freedom" of a land occupied by the Soviet terror.

The things that gave prisoners a sense of security were things I came to know well also. There was, for instance, the infinite, patient attention paid to the division of food. This was particularly painstaking and meaningful in the cells occupied by prisoners who helped with the serving of food from cell to cell, as I did many times.

During the serving of, say, barley broth, the prisoner-server would have little trouble in saving a cupful or so at the bottom of the bucket. This he could bring back to his cell, where, with as much care as a diamond merchant uses in sorting gems, the men would separate the grains of barley. Equal numbers of grains went to each cell mate. If a single grain remained at the end of the count, the server might claim it.

There was also the matter of filth. It preoccupied everyone. To our Soviet guards, cleanliness was of little concern. A guard to whom it was, stood out as an oddity. For the most part, the guards were like the soldiers who had streamed into Dresden to rape and burn and steal. They were dirty, ill clad, and untroubled by their condition. Few showed any familiarity with modern plumbing. In the prison toilets they scattered filthy toilet paper about the floor. Often they laughed at the toilets, like children seeing a strange, impractical toy for the first time.

Although necessity brought the guards to the prison bathrooms, they had a choice when it came to bathing in the prison tubs. By and large, they exercised this by staying away. There was a tub for the guards on every floor, but when a guard used it, word passed like a joke from cell to cell and the prisoners conjectured why the cleansing had been necessary.

Conjectures were coupled to the fact, learned from the ribald jokes of the guards as well as from prisoners who had spent time in the infirmary, that most of the guards had venereal diseases.

For practically all the prisoners, however, the chance to take a bath once a week was very important. My father and I, along with the few others who had survived the starvation regime, had waited six months or more for that day, December 28, 1945, when for the first time soap was distributed, a bath was made available, and we had shaves and haircuts. For the first time we could wash the bundle of stained and rotten rags which we called underclothes.

Bathing was so important to us that we could even

manage to live with the typically Soviet bathing regulations. No matter how many men were confined in a cell, from the luxurious three or four in my case to the ten to twenty in some others, only one tubful of water was permitted for each cell. For the last man in the tub, this meant stepping into a mildly tepid mud that reeked of body dirt. A prisoner not hardened to the system sometimes became ill as he stepped into the tub—and this usually put an end to bathing for the members of his cell.

To me, using the filthy tub water for bathing was as absurd as it was repulsive. The drinking water we got in our cells was the best for "spot cleaning." The water of the tub was more suitable for washing clothes.

We were permitted now to have our long, matted hair cut. Barbering was one of the miscellaneous skills my father had picked up when he first came to America as a Seventh Day Adventist missionary during the Depression. He practiced it before he took up his highly successful camera business.

When he told the guards of his skill he was quickly appointed to the prison barbering staff. This gave us a perfect chance to meet and talk regularly. My father became an encyclopedia of prison information.

One thing we learned through him was the interchangeability of guards and guarded in the Soviet world. My father had met the man who had been in charge of our arrest, the MVD officer Stepanenko. He was no longer an MVD officer. Now he was a prisoner, like us, in Münchenerplatz prison. He had been jailed as a direct result of his role in our arrest. From our home, where we kept a reserve stock, protected from possible air raids, Stepanenko had confiscated six hundred cameras. Then, as he explained freely, he had put the cameras on the black market. He was performing, after all, a simple equation in black-market economics. But he had been caught at it—possibly by a superior who felt *he* should have had the black-market concession for the cameras.

Stepanenko was not the only MVD officer on the prisoner list. The former chief of the prison was now a prisoner himself.

It was a mark of how complete a world our prison was that when a former prison chief or MVD officer became a prisoner there was no feeling of vengeance toward him. The prisoners accepted him as they would any prisoner, realizing, perhaps, that Communists are all captives of a system more rigid even than prison. When they in turn were imprisoned, they moved from one world to another with singular good feelings, it seemed. They showed an earthy, peasant indifference to their state.

While this was true of those who were jailed for graft or theft, crimes that meant little to their superiors, I was later to see that Russians imprisoned for political crimes quaked with terror. Stepanenko accepted with a shrug his seven-year sentence for black-market activities; had he passed an indiscreet remark about the regime, he would have been put to death.

In January 1946, six months after my arrival at the prison, I was given my first regular job: carrying water jugs and buckets and sweeping the prison corridors. My assignment came about, oddly enough, through Stepanenko, the same who had been in charge of our arrest.

During a regrouping of the prisoners, Stepanenko was put in charge of allocating new cell positions. Our relations with him were wholly without bitterness on either side, and he volunteered to place me as close to my father as possible. His efforts landed me in a cell adjacent to my father which was reserved for working prisoners. My assignment to that cell brought me onto the work rolls.

After two months of carrying water I fell heir to a new kind of job, a job that probably was the direct cause of my not leaving the Soviet prison system for nine years. I was to keep the prison records, and the work began when the guards brought a great stack of ledger books, writing materials, blanks, and other items. I thenceforward kept track of all prisoners, of which prisoners were in which cells, of their work assignments, of the reasons (if any) for their arrest, of the names of the MVD investigating officers, dates of interrogation, and other related data.

To do all this, and to continue with my old job of food helper, I had to make a daily round of the entire prison, with its approximately seven hundred inmates.

Under Russian management, the records had become an almost hopeless tangle of misfilings and incomplete information. My administrative training at the camera factory enabled me, however, to set up the records properly and quickly. Each day, as the records assumed better shape and I learned a little more about interrogations, charges, and the execution of prisoners, I was digging myself deeper into prison. I was becoming indispensable.

5 DEATH WAS A DAY-BY-day statistic in my bookkeeping at Münchenerplatz prison. Regularly I received a list of prisoners who were being ordered to appear before the prison court. The lists were written in red ink, in keeping with the official color motif of the Soviet court system. Everything about the system is red. Red cloths cover the court tables. Red hangings muffle the rooms.

At Münchenerplatz, the red-draped room used for court proceedings was kept fairly dark. A long table, covered with a red cloth, dominated the room, and at this table the three-man court seated itself. The MVD court members were a lieutenant colonel, a major, and a captain. During the court sessions two candles burned in front of the lieutenant colonel.

Trials were not held here. Trials were not held anywhere. There was only the reading of charges and the sentencing. A prisoner was brought into the courtroom, the door was closed behind him, and he was made to stand with his back against the door, fifteen feet away from the long table. Behind the flickering candles, the lieutenant colonel would read the charges and the sentence. An interpreter standing beside the prisoner would repeat the words in the language of the "criminal," who then was told to step forward to the table and sign his approval. He had been told that, if he did not care to sign, his refusal would not be held against him. But he need not worry; if he didn't sign, "someone else will."

The entire paperwork of the sentencing was prepared in advance; it was merely a matter of reading to the prisoner the list of crimes and investigations, then sentencing him. Whatever the charges or the sentence, the same procedure obtained. With mechanical informality, a man was sentenced to a few years in prison, to a life of slavery, or to death.

I came to realize that among the court members there

was a sincere indifference to the sentences. With some, the indifference was that of tribal Asia, where death is no more meaningful than a leak in a sod roof. Others had the trained attitude that death simply was a Soviet instrument of correction. It was the highest form of social hygiene, not unlike burning away a slum area or cauterizing a wound. These men felt no passion in sentencing people to death. They merely were snapping off a light switch.

On two days in June 1946 the sentencing was particularly memorable. The guard brought me the lists, on which as usual I wrote the cell numbers of the prisoners. Each day there were between twenty and thirty names in red; all, whatever the charges, were sentenced to death. The punishments would ordinarily have been varied to fit the crimes; but on those two days the members of the court were hopelessly drunk.

I knew little about theoretical Marxism at that time, but in this attitude toward death I sensed the gulf that separated these MVD officers from the Christian civilization to whose extinction they are committed. They believe that man is an animal, no more. To kill a man is no more significant than to kill a highly trained horse or a cow. If the beast becomes unmanageable, it is killed. If the man-beast becomes unmanageable, he is killed.

Although death sentences were passed every court day, the executions were carried out once a month. This was more efficient than shooting the people one by one, as sentenced.

A prisoner sentenced to death was put on half rations; since humans are animals, there is little sense in giving full rations to one that is about to be destroyed.

The squad assigned to bring the prisoners to the place of execution consisted of a junior-grade MVD lieutenant and two enlisted guards. Their procedure was standard-ized and, like the sentencing itself, almost casual. When the guards came to a cell where a sentenced prisoner was, they ordered him to remove his clothes. In some cases they forced him to take off everything, in others, an under-shirt might be worn. Clothes that were taken from pris-oners were heaped on the corridor floor. A guard would poke through the piles and pick out the good articles. The rest were turned over to me to distribute.

While the undressing went on, guards and officer would joke and laugh, usually over what they thought the pris-oners might do to their underwear if permitted to wear it to their death. What a waste of laundering it would be, they laughed.

In that joking was summed up a startling difference between these guards and the Nazi death squads about which those prisoners who had known both sometimes spoke. The Nazis, they said, killed viciously, because they were convinced that the people being killed were actually their enemies. The Russians killed because, almost liter-ally, a number had been drawn from a hat, because some meaningless document in some meaningless proceedings had said to snuff out the candle. No ferocity attended the executions. The reasons for the killings were as remote and irrelevant to the Russian guards as was the concept of death itself. Their joking, then, was not forced. When they patted a prisoner's shoulder, the action came easily. Life had to end for certain integers in the state table of statistics. That's all, comrade. Nothing personal, comrade.

Horribly, the laughter of the guards marked those days more than did the sounds of the killings themselves.

The process of execution, about which the guards some-times boasted because it was so "humane," was simplicity itself. After a condemned prisoner had undressed, he was led to a partly shattered wing of the prison. As he rounded the corner into a corridor of the wing, a guard shot him in the back of the head. It was "humane," because it came without warning.

As each prisoner was shot, his body was dragged to the end of the corridor. By the end of a day's killing, a stack of sprawling bodies, naked or in undershirts, stood in the dark and dirty hall. A guard doused the bodies with gasoline and tossed on a match. The flames from the pyre made a light that often was seen by prisoners in other parts of the building. A guard, if questioned, would explain that trash was being burned.

As the smoke from the burning bodies drifted from the execution corridor into other parts of the prison, it was difficult to make anyone believe that it was anything but exactly what it was. On execution days, in many cells not even the pitiful scraps that passed for rations were eaten.

One execution day the flames from the cindering corpses rose higher than usual, perhaps because of an extravagant drenching with fuel. From the burning bodies the flames licked up and caught the wood trim, moldings, and sashes of the corridor. The guards, idly watching the blaze till now, ran for aid. My helper and I were called out to haul a hose up to extinguish the flames, but we were not permitted to turn the corner into the corridor itself. The guards carried the hose into the death corridor and flushed the flames from the grisly torch they had set.

To some prisoners the walk in the corridor probably was a relief, as humane as the Russians said it was. These were the prisoners who had been tortured. For some time, I had known only the sounds of torture. But I learned, as I came to know more about the prison during my records-keeping job, what it was that produced the shrieks and sobs.

The most common form of torture was the beating with strips of thick, lead-wrapped, electric installation pipe, covered with heavy insulation. They were about one third of an inch wide and two feet long. It was not uncommon to see guards strolling around with these whips in their hands. In the interrogation rooms, however, the pipes were put to their harshest use.

The questioning involved the victim, an investigating MVD officer, and an interpreter. Oddly enough, it also usually involved the proposition that the victim was innocent of whatever charge the Communists had brought against him and to which they wanted him to confess. The regularity with which this was true seemed at first a nightmare, without rhyme or reason. I soon learned, though, how sensible it was, from the Communist point of view. If a person was indeed guilty of something, the Communists usually had little trouble proving it. At least, they had facts enough at hand to warrant a passable charge. But if the person was innocent, the whip would pound and lash the desired "guilt" into the person's back muscles, nerve fibers, mind, and consciousness.

I helped to carry one of the beaten prisoners to his cell. He had been whipped with his shirt on. His skin was laid open from the ridge of his shoulders all the way to his belt line, and the shirt had been ground into the raw meat of his back. For an hour, with the doctor who also was a prisoner, I picked bits of shredded cloth from the wounds, trying always to pick bloody cloth rather than the slivers of split red flesh. When we had finished cleaning his back, we wrapped him in strips of toilet paper,

33

the prison dispensary's gesture toward providing medicine for the man.

More complex and subtle, and I always have thought more damaging, was the torture of the disinfecting cabinet. This was a large, boilerlike metal cabinet in which, under the German prison administration, mattresses had been disinfected—a cleanliness undreamed of in any Russian-administered prison at that time.

Prisoners being moved through the corridors or going about prison work were able to see this looming presence, with its high-pressure steam pipes and valves. What they did not know, if they were new and had not circulated among the veteran prisoners, was that the disinfecting tank was no longer connected to receive steam. It was these new prisoners that went to the tank for their torture.

A prisoner was thrown into the tank by guards who were being purposefully rough to intimate that severe punishment was underway. Inside, the terrified prisoner watched the steel hatch swing shut and heard the booming clang as the locking mechanism turned and the bolts seated themselves in their slots.

In the total interior darkness, the prisoner could only expect a searing jet of steam or a choking cloud of poisonous gas to be pumped in. And so he would be left for a full day or two, the door never being opened.

After this ordeal, several prisoners were taken from the tank completely mad. No person ever emerged without serious nervous consequences. Most came out of it with hair turned gray. All were willing to confess to whatever the Communists wished them to confess.

Another psycho-physical torture method was used of which I had heard, although I never saw the place where it was carried out. I have, however, seen prisoners brought back from it. A deep pit, possibly used at one time as part of a drainage or garbage-disposal system in the prison, was filled with water to knee height. The victim was placed in this pit, standing with his clothes on. Every half hour a pail of water was thrown over him. First there was the tense waiting, and then the wet shock. Both grew progressively worse. As the water level rose, by pailfuls, from knees, to hips, to waist, a slow horror welled within the man. Finally he was ready to confess anything that was expected of him.

The very system of Communist arrests inevitably led to a system of torture that was as much mental as physical. Arrests were made to terrorize the citizens, in sweeping, indiscriminate raids. Men were arrested as they walked the streets, as they dined or sat in the homes of friends. They were arrested anywhere, anytime, without explanation. Everyone in the city was kept poised on the edge of terror.

There was a plan to it all, and it was remarkably effective even beyond its terrorizing results. When a load of prisoners newly yanked from home and street were thrown into cells, the first topic of speculation naturally was "Why was I arrested?" They would search their memories for minor infractions and even for unvoiced thoughts antagonistic to the Communists. A cell full of prisoners might talk for hours about these things, elaborating upon point after point, seeking always a clue to their arrest. There was, of course, no clue. But in every cell was a Communist police informer, patiently listening as the prisoners spelled out possible grounds for Communist charges. It was the unfortunates who could find absolutely no reason whatever for their arrests that were passed on to the body-and-mind-racking torments of lash and tank and pit.

A torture of humiliation for us all was the regular weekly search, when guards would sweep through the prison and pick over our personal belongings. These had been thrown to the floor, and contraband or any article that might seem desirable to the guards was taken. We then were forced to kneel down and sort out our pitiful belongings. To see the paltry scraps of one's only personal life—shreds of soap, a wad of toilet paper, a saved crust, an extra pair of torn socks—thrown on the floor and then to have to scramble for them was a brutalizing experience. I came to dread it as others must have dreaded an expected new ordeal with the whip.

The severity of these searches depended upon what day of the week they were carried out. In midweek they were routine and without incident. The guards came in, belongings were heaped, and the recovery scramble began.

But if an additional search was held, on Friday or Saturday, beatings and other abuses were added. This was a result of the MVD indoctrination course. Every Friday, all MVD officers and guards were assembled for ideological lectures. After the lectures, the guards toured the cells, grabbing prisoners at random, asking incredible questions, and administering beatings to any who could not answer—and no one ever could. If, during these sessions, a search was ordered, every cell could expect a hard time. The guards would take special pains to rip and tear the articles they threw to the floor. They walked over things, crushing, perhaps, a treasured pair of glasses or other breakable object. When prisoners stooped to pick up their things, the guards might kick them. Prisoners were thrown bodily from cells and smashed against walls.

There seemed to be only one defense at these times of special abuse. Prisoners who cringed before the guards were kicked, beaten, spat upon. Prisoners who suddenly turned on the guards and struck out at them were taken away for hours of extreme torture or were killed. But those men fared best who went through the indignities calmly and stoically, without cringing or losing their tempers, apparently with an inner conviction that the Communist animal terror could not break them. The Communists could not cope with men, it seemed to me, who insisted on remaining more than the animals which Communists regard men to be.

Day after day I witnessed the torment and terror dealt out to my fellow prisoners. I, myself, being too useful to be submitted to more than the common humiliations, never knew when my turn might suddenly come. My work kept me busy from 7:00 A.M. to past midnight, and I had little time to let my thoughts wander too far back or too far ahead. I was aware, of course, that I never could leave this prison without undergoing the investigational process. On the one hand I dreaded to see it come, because it was bound to involve terror and ill treatment. On the other hand, I preferred an end, with fear, to fear without end. All that could save me from either was a change in system, but what prospect was there of that?

The time came when a wave of efficiency swept through Münchenerplatz prison. The fact that prisoners had been there for months without sentencing had finally been brought to the commandant's attention by an aide. This aide, ironically, had been thrown into a cell for a time as punishment for some indiscretion. It was then that I had a chance to talk with him and mention the growing backlog of unsentenced prisoners. That I, for instance, had been in for thirteen months came as a distinct surprise to him. When he was released, he relayed my information to the commandant. Within a few days all my records were ordered ready for inspection.

MVD General Klebov himself showed up to handle the inspection. He set up office in a storeroom, and through one whole night long lines of prisoners stood, waiting for an interview with Klebov's staff as the sentencing procedure was reviewed. After that, a new system of interrogations was established: they were carried out in shifts. Within two weeks all but 250 prisoners had either been executed or sent to concentration camps to serve sentences elsewhere.

The thought that my turn to be interrogated was inevitably approaching was constantly with me. When it came, it would mean execution or transfer, I could not decide which. I knew it would be one or the other, of course, for my keeping of all the prison personnel records made me aware that the Communists hardly would let me off scot free. I had personally checked the files of 21,000 prisoners at Münchenerplatz, and I knew that murder and torture were the most common alternatives.

When my turn for questioning under the speed-up system did arrive, I knew that the Communists were well aware of how much I had seen. It was little use trying to pretend, as I so earnestly did pretend, that the records-keeping job had made no serious impact on me.

The questioning officer went through a maze of routine questions. Then, with a casualness that was obvious, he asked what I had heard of my mother and brother and what was going on in our factory. When I tried to avoid giving a straight answer, he interrupted me:

"John, you know exactly what the situation is. You

38

speak to every newcomer here when you make out his records. You know where your mother is and you know exactly what is being produced in your father's factory."

No accusations were laid against me, and on sending me back into the prison hall the interrogator told me that they merely wanted to look into my case a little more deeply.

A few days later the duty sergeant came to me and said, "That's all now, John. Hand over all the papers and we'll find someone else to do this work."

The thought came to me that he might be working to get me locked up again, for I once had warned him about robbing our cells and taking essential property from the prisoners for his personal use.

I was left to myself, but not for long. At 6:00 o'clock on the morning of August 31, 1946, a guard came to my cell, pulled me out of sleep, and said, "Take all your things, John. You're going away."

"Where to?" was my immediate question.

"You probably know better than I do where all those transports go," he replied. Then, as he looked at my puzzled face, he must have known what I was thinking. "Yes," he said, "your father is going with you."

This, under the circumstances, was a happy surprise. Usually they liked to separate relatives and send them to different camps.

The guard led me along the hall and down the steps to the first floor. As I passed a certain door, I stopped for a second to look at it once again. Hundreds of men had walked through it naked, or nearly so, in their last minute of life. A few others, including myself, also had passed through that door occasionally, accompanied by guards.

We were looking for prisoners' old clothes, blankets, sheets, aprons, and other articles. That part of the building was quite destroyed.

Once, I came a little closer to the execution department than prisoners were permitted to do, but the guard was friendly and he let me look. I saw only a smoke-stained end of a corridor. I acted as if I were not interested, and I searched from cell to cell for clothing. Blood-stained rags I found which, variously, were once the uniforms of prisoners of war, Danish streetcar conductors, and Dutch postoffice clerks. Also there were civilian clothes, as bloody as the rest, no doubt remnants of the closing days of World War II, when bloodshed was greatest. One system did not differ too much from another.

I recalled another time, also, when I passed through that door. I came to the bombed-out end and looked out over a pile of rubble at people walking along the street only yards away. The guard was in another wing, and I could have jumped over the rocks and run out of sight in seconds, but I realized at once that, in reprisal, my father would have been put to death in the smoke-stained corridor.

As on this last day of August I looked at that door, the guard stepped toward me and said in schoolbook German, nodding in the direction of the exit, "Schnell ausgang!"

6 I HAD TWO BLANKETS, three sheets, a set of work clothes, my business suit, a pair of slippers I had made from scraps of discarded blankets, and my shoes. Secretly, I had some inch-long bits of lead from the pencils I had used in my prison job and some tightly folded bits of paper. Finally, I had a short piece of string. I used this as a belt, tying together the front loops of my trousers with it.

A guard brought me to the main hall, where other prisoners—men and women—were waiting. There was no talking. The people sat on their bundles, if they had any. If not, they stood uneasily or sat on the floor. No one looked at another prisoner. No one knew what was going to happen. No one, by an expression on the face or by a glance, wanted to intimate the smallest speculation as to where he was going to be sent. It was the suspended animation of change in a prison. Everyone was hanging over the unknown, wishing perhaps that he could wait forever and never have to learn what might lie ahead.

The guards searched our belongings (missing my paper and pencil leads) and lined us up against the far wall. As the line grew, other prisoners were brought in. One was my father. I tried not to watch as his things were spilled on the floor, rooted through, and pitched back to him. He joined the line, and when the searching was finished, about forty men and women were there, silent and waiting.

We were taken by bus to the prison camp at Mühlberg, forty miles north along the Elbe. My first sight of the place told me that henceforth I would be seeing Soviet prison life stripped to its essentials, without any of the "refinements" offered by a city prison such as Dresden's.

As the bus slowed, approaching the wire boundaries of the Mühlberg prison camp, we could see a huge wooden cart being pulled from the camp toward an adjoining field by about fifty prisoners. On the cart was a vast wooden tub, about twenty feet long. From the high windows of the bus we could see that it was filled to the top with human excrement. I learned later that the reeking mass was from the latrines within the camp. Every few days the tub was filled from individual pails and hauled to the field for dumping into an open pit. There, as I was to find out, relatives of prisoners would wait—after bribing the guards—for a chance to pass on packages to those inside the camp.

The method was simple. The packages were tossed into the excrement tub. When it was hauled back inside the camp, prisoners expecting packages would claw down into the bottom of the tub to find their gifts. The reeking, dripping condition of the packages made no difference to them. New prisoners, sometimes, were sickened. But they got used to it after a while.

As we dismounted from the bus, inside the prison area, it was obvious that some of the prisoners had virtually lost the ability to walk without specific directions being given to them. There was no question about where we were supposed to go: a group of MVD officers waited for

42

us outside a prison building. But most prisoners just milled together, soundlessly, eyes downcast, rather than follow the guards toward the waiting officers. They had to be shoved and shouted into line and on their way.

I realized once again that death was the least thing to fear under the conditions of captivity by the Reds.

Just inside the compound there were long wooden benches. On these we spread our belongings for another search. This time a few of the better blankets and shirts disappeared. Not all the searching was done by MVD personnel. Prisoners, wearing red brassards, officiously scattered our belongings also. These were the trusted prisoners, to whom the MVD assigned certain duties. It was easy to see why they were trusted, for they were men who had been picked up as criminals and wanted to wash off their guilt. By cooperating with the MVD, they would win the rewards of power, extra rations, and earlier release —if they wanted it.

After the search we were conducted to barracks 32. We were to have our first experience of barracks prison, as contrasted with cell prison. The building, of rough planking, was about 220 feet long and perfectly bare inside. A few windows lighted the place. Along the whitewashed walls wooden shelves ran, about six feet wide. These were our beds. One shelf went along the wall at a height of about three feet, another about three feet above that. Wooden ladders, fastened at intervals, gave access to the upper tier. There was space for about 150 men on the shelves; our group, when the women were separated, numbered about thirty. Everyone took a luxuriously large space on the lower bench.

Two coal-burning stoves warmed the barracks. Dividing the barracks down the center was a partitioned area with a concrete floor; in this was a long trough for washing clothes and a space for serving food.

No. 32 was a quarantine barracks, and our stay there lasted ten days. My father and I were assigned to No. 10, which was jammed. There was space for us only on the top shelf, and even so we slept touching the men on either side of us.

One compensation made these first days at Mühlberg pass rather easily. My father and I had hours in which to talk together. We did not speak any more of release, beyond comparing notes on past questionings. Those to which my father had been subjected, he said, emphasized a line of interrogation that was both frustrating and revealing. Time after time, MVD questioners had doggedly tried to break what to them was the "mystery" of how my father had come to be the owner of a large and obviously prosperous factory in Germany. Clearly, the Russians thought it was part of a plot, for nothing in their experiences corresponded to a situation such as this.

My father was born in Germany as Charles Spanknobel. He changed the name to Noble after becoming an American citizen. He was a shoemaker by trade, but his preference clearly lay toward the activities of the Seventh Day Adventist Church, of which his parents were members. As a young man, therefore, he enrolled in an Adventist missionary school. He was graduated just in time to be drafted by the German army for service in the first World War. In keeping with the policy of his church, however, he refused combat service and was ordained a minister. At one point he was assigned to Switzerland as a missionary. There, my brother George was born. From Switzerland, with George and my mother, he was sent to

44

America to preach in the Adventist churches. To pay him adequately for this, however, was too great a luxury for the beleaguered church, and my mother, to help out, capitalized on her hobby, photography, and found a job in a photo finisher's shop in Detroit. The Depression was on, business was bad, and the proprietor wanted to close up. My mother, the last employee to stay on, was prepared to do what she could to keep the business going. The proprietor was killed in an accident in the West, and the business was scheduled to be sold. My father managed to scrape money together to buy it, and they put their heads together to try and make a go of it.

The venture worked out well, and by the early 1930s we were perfectly solvent. My father was even able to go back to Germany for treatment of a serious gall-bladder ailment. While there, he invested wisely in industrial properties. In 1937 he bought the KW-Praktiflex camera factory in Dresden. A year later he brought the entire family over so that they could be with him while he got things started. Also, with this arrangement, he would be able to complete a projected two- or three-year treatment of his disability. Then war trapped us.

That was all there was to it, but it was beyond the concepts of the MVD. They were convinced that we were in league with the Nazis, with the American warmongers, with somebody sinister. How otherwise could one own a factory?

7

MÜHLBERG WAS LIKE A vast sewer, with rotten things, the prisoners, floating in it. Rottenness seemed to touch almost everybody.

The filthiness of the prison and its inmates caused boils and lesions, which, according to rumor, could be cured if scraped and then laved with human urine. It was not uncommon to see a man hunched at the end of the trough that carried urine from the latrine to an open cesspool outside. The man had so positioned himself that the urine would flow over his sores. The "cure" often developed into a horror of infections.

Sexual practices, both normal and abnormal, were crude and animalistic. Homosexuality was rife throughout all the camp and among both sexes, particularly the younger people. When an entire barracks building had been turned over, as an experiment, to an indoctrination course in communism, the young men whom the Russians hoped to instruct demonstrated that they had no interest in any ism but homosexualism. They were brutal in their performance, unmanageable as a group, and immune to instruction.

Mühlberg's "normal" sexual activity centered for the most part in barracks 12, which was used as a storehouse and a sewing room for the repair of flour sacks. By and large, it was very well managed. I had fleeting opportu-

CAMP Officers' Quarters **MÜHLBERG**

Main Gate

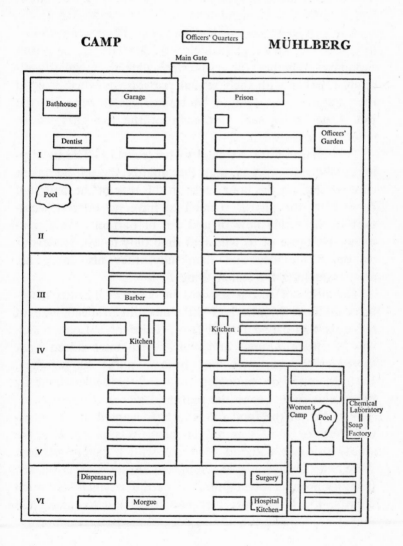

nities of visiting it, to pick up onions and other store supplies, having volunteered to work in the food-supply system of the camp. Scores of other prisoners, I can attest, had time for more extended visits.

Ten girls were assigned to barracks 12 as seamstresses to repair the flour sacks which were a vital item of prison economy. Whether the girls were picked by guards already familiar with their sexual prowess, or whether good raw material was sent to be trained, as it were, on the job, I never learned. But each of the ten girls was a whore of consequence.

Two guards were assigned to barracks 12. The unvarying daily routine was that the guards should be taken care of first, on the flour sacks in the rear of the building. After that, the guards seemed to have no interest whatever in the traffic flow in and out of barracks 12. Fortunately for those of us who had time only to eat, to devour an onion hungrily and thankfully, they also were lax about watching for stolen things.

The price of sexual services in barracks 12 was measured in food. Money had little meaning. Indeed, one of the girls was called Drittel Brot, Third of a Loaf, which was her price. Onions and flour, which were stored right there, in the barracks, had little standing as currency. Pastries, made on smuggled time with smuggled flour by the prison cooks, were the real gold pieces.

Yet, for all the food that the girls wanted, it was obvious that sex itself was an independent appetite. For the sturdy prisoner with no food but with a raging passion, there was always a girl willing to throw herself on the flour sacks free. Sometimes, as partial payment for such charity, the lusting prisoner had to submit to letting the

48

other girls watch, and perhaps joke or comment on his performance.

One of the leaders of the sewing circle was known as the False Countess, because she boasted of having been arrested during her wedding to a Polish count. She was quite ugly but was possessed of an energy that apparently impressed the Russian guards. Indeed, given the choice between a beautiful woman who was passive or, perhaps, who required persuasion, and one who, like the False Countess, was ugly but shy of underthings and great for sitting on steps, the Russians almost invariably chose the indelicate but available.

The False Countess was not only available but aggressively so. With another of the barracks-12 girls who was nicknamed, for subtle anatomical reasons, The Horse, she was arrested for rape on the charge of a guard who said that the pair had grabbed him, thrown him to the floor, and ravished him as he made his inspection of the barracks. After three days in the camp prison the two girls began a thriving practice among the guards there. Women guards then were placed at their cell. The two girls escaped. Their first act was to fling themselves into a pond and call for help. A young prisoner working on the bank splashed in after them, but before he had gotten them out of the shallow water, the girls had torn his pants off.

Once, when I went into barracks 12 for supplies, I saw a new girl there, British and quite good looking. On subsequent trips I noticed that she always was hard at work sewing. She seemed an amazing exception to the table of organization in barracks 12. The reason for this I soon learned. In another prison she had been saved from death by a Russian woman doctor, who had later taken her on as a maid. After a few weeks, the Russian explained an additional service she wanted the girl to perform, namely, to whip her. The Russian woman's sexual abnormality consisted of a desire to be whipped. After a while, the British girl came to share it. Hence her distinctive conduct in barracks 12.

The commandant of the prison was a proper person for the job, a sick man in a sick place. His delight was theatrical entertainment, but it was far from a healthy delight. Prisoners with entertainment background were carefully screened out of each incoming roster. If their act or skill required props, guards would be sent to fetch these.

The director of a Leipzig nightclub was in charge of camp entertainment. Each night he delivered a stageful of acts for the commandant and his staff. Jugglers, singers, dancers, anyone who could perform in any way were ordered on stage. Some sang or danced in their filthy prison clothes. Next might come a ballerina, her legs hunger-shrunken to knotted sticks but her *tutu* as neat as the petals of a flower. The horrid contrasts on the stage didn't seem to bother the commandant. At each act, good, bad, or indifferent, he applauded along with his staff.

That wasn't the worse part, though. Behind the Russians in the theater each night were rows of prisoners, admitted to give the theater a gala, packed look. Besides stinking, the prisoners were starving. But nothing mattered to the commandant; not the prisoners, some dying, who performed on the stage, nor the skeletal ranks in the rows behind.

After a while, the commandant felt the urge for a new, brick theater to replace the old wooden structure. Prisoners, of course, built it. Several died at the work. All were beaten to speed things along. But the commandant had his shows, each night.

Carefully sewn into one of the belt loops of my pants was a 1000-mark note that I had managed to keep with me from the time of our arrest. My father and I heard that cigarets could be bought from the guards if one had money. Neither of us smoked but we knew that with cigarets we could barter for food. One entire day's ration of bread could be purchased from the camp bakery's black market for one cigaret.

The 1000-mark note began to represent a storehouse waiting to be tapped. My father and I had never even tried to bribe our way past a head waiter, but now we began to concentrate on converting money into bread.

One by one, my father and I casually questioned prisoners. Did anyone know of a way to get cigarets for German currency? We found our man. The going rate, he said, was one mark per cigaret—but a 1000-mark transaction was too great a risk. The source of the cigarets? A Russian guard, of course.

Finally we arrived at a workable agreement. We would get 200 cigarets and the guard would obtain change. The go-between was to get 200 marks. For a moment we worried about the possibility that the guard or the go-between would simply take our money and that would be that. But we realized that such an action would be short-sighted for shrewd businessmen, and the guards were just that. Running the risk of spoiling a long-term lucrative traffic for one quick profit would be absurd. The notion that Communist adherence to anti-capitalist principle would hinder such a transaction never occurred to us: so far, we had not met a single guard who seemed in any way involved with Communist *ideology*. They were simply

51

guards. They could have been guarding the prisoners of any system, capitalist, Communist, Socialist, Fascist, and would have behaved the same.

The day for the big trade arrived. We turned over the 1000-mark note. The go-between went off to meet his Russian friend. He was back at dusk. He had our cigarets all right, but he also had a new arrangement. Instead of change, which we really didn't want, we would get all our money in cigarets, over a period of months. The first installment of 200 was handed over on the spot.

"Think of it," my father said as he picked up the cardboard box in which the cigarets were stacked. "There's two thirds of a year's bread ration in that box." It seemed a bit comic.

By October it seemed less comic and more grimly important than ever. Rations were cut in half. The German army stores which had been used to feed the prison so far had finally run out. Now the food had to come from the Red army itself, and that military colossus simply didn't have enough to waste on prisoners.

When the cut was announced, most of us blamed it first of all on Russian arrogance—on not wanting to waste Russian food on foreigners. Those of us who remained in the Russian prison system soon discovered a different reason. It was part of the harsh, hollow truth of the Soviet. The country is insufficient in all respects, in food, in production of its resources, in industry. There simply isn't enough of anything—except political indoctrination and power—to go around. The Soviet Union is a land of shortages and of hungers.

It is strong only in its ability to awe the rest of the world and to bluff its way to a position of dominance. For the prisoners, it was an academic question as to *how* the

52

Soviet was strong enough to hold its prisoners from every land on earth. It was enough that it could be done and was being done.

When the food cut was put into effect, the cigaret price of bread jumped by four. Still, the cigaret fortune we had acquired kept us going rather well. Some 400 cigarets had been delivered to us by Christmas time, and we felt we could splurge on a bonus of fifty to a cook who promised to provide extra rations every day, beginning with Christmas dinner.

It was while we were waiting for our black-market treat that I saw the procession of the dead through the camp. It was an extraordinary march. Seventy-two persons who had died on Christmas Eve were being carried by other prisoners to a trenchlike grave outside the prison area.

I looked at each of the corpses being carried past, and at each of the prisoners carrying them. It was just light enough to see each man clearly; between the features of the living and those of the dead I could hardly distinguish: shrunken faces, empty eyes, and gray, ashen skin.

The procession passed by the only tree in camp, a conifer in front of the prison staff building. The tree had seemed a symbol of Christmas. Seeing it now, as the dead passed by it, I became sickened by the thought of our Christmas dinner. For every one of our black-market cigarets, I realized, we had taken food that might have gone to someone else—perhaps to one of the dead men I had just seen.

I spoke to my father about it, and we agreed to cancel our black-market arrangements. The privilege we had bought had not been bought with cigarets, really. It had been bought with greed and thoughtlessness.

I ate alone that night in the stable, where the prison's

work animals were kept. There were grain husks spilled on the floor. They seemed more than enough.

8 RISING ABOVE THE squalor and even degeneracy of Mühlberg was the dedication of two groups of men, the clergy and the physicians. The Catholic priests and Protestant ministers did far more than attend, under greatest difficulties, to their proper churchly duties—masses said quickly in the corner of a barracks, a sermon preached and a hymn softly sung behind the latrines. The priests and ministers performed their greatest work, I think (for those who had not become oblivious, rutting, feeding animals), by their humility. No job was too mean for them. To the humility of each job, whether amid the filth of the latrines or the mud outdoors, these men brought the sure and tremendous dignity of their faith.

If there was one species of armor, and one alone, that I could unhesitatingly say would turn the assaults of brainwashing and misery and terror of slave and prison camps, I would say that that armor was a sure knowledge of God. Without that rocklike faith, men or women entering Red slavery become no more than what the Communists say all men are, animals.

Another strong force of dedication was that of the doctors in the camp. In their work they expressed in the highest and noblest degree the oath that all doctors have sworn to live by. In Mühlberg, the imprisoned German doctors sustained and mended the wretched threads of life with, literally, love, bare hands, and kitchen knives. The sacrifices they made were beyond reason and public responsibility. They were the expressions of individual charity in the true, loving sense of that word.

Our prison diet alone would barely maintain life in a strong person of good constitution. For the weak, aged, and infirm, the diet was a death sentence. Yet many of these people lived, walking skeletally on the edge of starvation and collapse. It was the doctors, with jury-rigged implements and medicines, who kept them in this world.

The doctors, as a group, had been permitted to take over the rooms which, under the German operation of Mühlberg, had been an infirmary but which, under the Russians, had become barracks and storage space. The Russians permitted this arrangement with the doctors through no humanitarian motives. Rather, they saw that they themselves might need medical attention, and the doctors attached to the Red army were trained to about the level of medical corpsmen or first-aid workers. They stood in open awe of the German doctors and were, sincerely, I think, anxious to learn from them. The Russians often spoke of their outstanding medical-research figures, but their boasts amounted to praise for a mere handful of men, which in all probability comprised the entire top level of Russian medicine. As in so much else of Russia's technology and science, there were only two levels—a top level of great excellence but representing a very few persons and a normal level of little skill comprising the vast majority.

(At Mühlberg, for instance, all prisoners with aeronautical-design experience were given a chance for extra rations by joining a research project. The prisoners were

55

given instruments and drawing tables and were told to work on certain design problems which, presumably, had already defeated Russia's sketchy technology. One prisoner who had only a meager training in aeronautical engineering was, nevertheless, able to fool the Russian supervisors completely and enjoy extra rations while doodling at his drawing board.)

If a Russian officer became ill, he knew that the only responsible medical treatment would be available from the German doctors. The Russian "doctors" were adequate, perhaps, for the enlisted personnel, but the officers were realistic enough to want genuine medical attention.

Despite the Russians' self-interest, however, there was pathetically little to turn over to the doctors for their use besides the space of the old infirmary. There were a very few old surgical instruments, one battered operating table, and a few stained cartons of medical supplies that had somehow escaped the Russians' systematic looting of all German medical installations.

Even with the scanty equipment at hand, however, the doctors turned the shambles into a hospital. It was not illness alone that they had to handle. There was the more insidious and prevalent plague of weakness and malnutrition. A foremost need was for proteins and vitamins to fill in the nutritional gaps of a sparse, starchy diet.

The proteins were obtained from human hair. Each day, bundles of hair, clipped from shaggy prisoners, were brought to the doctors. With the pressure-and-heat systems that they had strung together out of old tubings and electrical coils and with the chipped residue of the infirmary's lab equipment, the doctors processed the hair into a protein extract.

For vitamin supplements, the doctors relied heavily upon pine needles. These were stripped from the trees brought into the camp for the preparation of ersatz wood-pulp bread.

My first experience inside the infirmary came in February. While climbing a stockroom ladder, carrying a 100-kilogram sack of grain, I slipped and fell, injuring my foot. When I found that I couldn't walk, I was taken to the infirmary. One of the doctors exclaimed, half jokingly, to see such a healthy specimen brought in. What impressed him was my weight. By working in the stockroom and availing myself of the perquisites of the job—an onion here, a potato there, a handful of grain—I had boosted my weight to a "fat" 100 pounds, a mere fifty pounds or so below my normal weight. Earlier, I had been down to ninety-five pounds, a more normal figure for the prison and a weight at which I later was to remain for many years.

While in the infirmary, waiting for my foot to heal, I was stricken with appendicitis. Before the opening of the infirmary, this would have been a death sentence. I knew now there was hope, although I also knew that if the doctors operated they would have to do so with instruments more suitable to a kitchen. But men who can distill life from hair and pine needles are somehow expected to be performers of magic in all circumstances.

I was taken into the operating room shortly after the first convulsion of pain flooded down my side. The room was spotlessly clean, even though its walls were chipped and flaked, its floor splintered and warped, and its windows gaping. A bare light bulb hung above the operating table. There were no such luxuries as sheets to hide the battered old table, its scabs of rust meticulously scraped off and its wheels and levers held in place by knots of wire and old nails.

The few instruments that had been left in the infirmary were lined up; beside them were the ones that the doctors had made themselves. Clamps to hold back incisions had been devised from strips of tin can, bent and hammered into shape, the jagged edges providing a grip. On the clamps, bits of string substituted for chains. Scalpels had been made from jackknives and saw blades, painstakingly ground and honed to the best edge they could hold.

Fortunately, there was a hypodermic needle among the left-over supplies. With this I was given a spinal anaesthetic. Only after the operation did I understand why the doctors had sounded so concerned as they asked me if the anaesthetic was working.

When the operation was over, the doctors told me the spinal anaesthetic had been part of a batch brought in by a Red officer on whom they had operated. They used a portion of it, having no way of knowing whether it was good or even how much to inject. The labels were so weathered that they couldn't be read, and there was only the Russian's word that it even *was* an anaesthetic.

The doctors also told me that I was the proud possessor of some of the first honest sutures they had been able to use since starting surgery in the camp. Previously, sutures had been fashioned from the thin wire of electrical heating coils, clipped and straightened. Mine had been made from catgut. More important, they confided, mine was the first operation that had been performed without any immediate complications.

These doctors, from some of the finest hospitals and research staffs in the world, seemed as proud of having

58

conquered the problems of kitchen-knife surgery, of keeping flies off open incisions, as if they had won a collective Nobel Prize. To the prisoners, they had won more precious prizes, many times over.

9

THE SLOW, TERRIBLE odyssey toward the Arctic and slavery began to move faster even before I had fully recovered from the operation.

Signs of change began to rustle in the camp like leaves before a storm. On the day of my release from the hospital, a gateway messenger picked me up and took me to the gate, and from there I was sent to the prison's special confinement dungeon. My pockets were emptied. Again a riveted door clanged shut on me. For the first day no one came to the cell except at feeding time, and then all I got for my "why?" was a mute shrug of the shoulders.

For the next three days the visits were more frequent but the answers just as nonexistent. Twenty or more times each day my cell door was opened by a guard—always a different one. The routine was the same. "German?" the guard would ask. "Amerikanitz," I would reply in one of the very few words of Russian I had learned.

Word had spread through the camp that an American was in the dungeon. All the guards wanted to see for themselves. I suppose that it was a great symbol, for them, of their fatherland's power. It was a great symbol of that power for the prisoners as well.

On the fourth day, an officer named Narajanov called me into the corridor. Almost mechanically he began to fire questions at me. When had I been in the city of Mühlberg? When had I been to Burgsdorf, the camp's railway station? When had I ever been outside the camp to go anywhere?

The answer to all was "never," and I had no idea why the questions even had been asked. They seemed meaningless. Narajanov grunted at my answers, shoved me back in the cell, and strode away.

For twenty-three days I was able to lie in the cell and wonder about the questions. There was little else to do. The cell measured six by three feet, the size of a closet. A cot took up almost all the floor space. The walls were a dead white, and outside the door a 400-watt bulb glared day and night until the white of the walls seemed to seep through every part of my brain.

After a while the attempt to ignore the light brought on a most acute form of awareness of its unblinking presence. No physical discomfort in the cell was nearly as bad.

Between the walls of each two cells there was a metal slot in which wood or coal fires could be built to heat the cells. Fires were got going in the slot about seven in the morning. By noon the walls were too hot to get near, and I gasped in the humid heat, wet with perspiration. In the evening the fires were permitted to go out, and the outer doors to the cell corridors were opened to let the freezing winds whip through. We had no blankets. Each night was a chattering, cold, huddled horror. Each day was a hot, heavy prelude to the freezing night.

On the twenty-third day, Narajanov ordered me

brought to the staff building. My knee, swollen as an after-math of the operation and the spinal injection, and un-exercised in the cell, made the walk to the building a tor-ture. The guard who accompanied me didn't even notice as I grunted and shuffled, almost dragging one leg. Most prisoners had some locomotive defect, from weakness or injury. Mine was just one of many.

In Narajanov's office I was amazed to hear exactly the same three questions that he had asked me in the corridor by my cell. Then, after the familiar grunt, he added one other: had I ever written to anyone outside the prison? With my astonished "no," he had me taken back to the barracks. I was "free." I was out of the dungeon and back to the normal world of the prison camp. And that was exactly the way I felt. All thoughts of *real* freedom had become fantasies.

This was freedom now. Being able to move more than six feet before facing a wall. Being able to speak to oth-ers. Being able to huddle beneath one's own blanket.

(Many months later, from another prisoner, and in an-other prison camp, I learned why I had been sent to the dungeon. A letter had come to the camp addressed to:

> Mr. Charles A. Noble
> and Mr. John H. Noble
> c/o Lt. Coln. Saisikov
> Camp No. —
> Muehlberg/Elbe
> Germany

I have never discovered the origin of that letter; all I know is that, according to the stamp, it came from the United States. But it is obvious why the letter should have disturbed the prison officials. It meant that someone, somewhere, was aware of our location. And, by the logic of a terror state, it was very dangerous that anyone should know the whereabouts of a man who handled more than 20,000 Soviet police dossiers in a German prison, someone who had been around to count the murders, the kidnapings, the tortures, and the starvations.)

As 1947 ended and I got back into the cocoon routine of a prisoner, there came the first evidence of a political fact of life that I was to notice many times afterward. Through the propaganda of the East German papers that were permitted to circulate through the prison we knew that the West had stiffened its back for a moment against the arrogance of the Soviet. Too, elections of a sort were to be held in East Germany—bayonet elections, to be sure, but elections that at least had to have some of the trappings of freedom.

The impact of these things on the prison was apparent. Food was received in better (if not copious) condition. Disciplinary raids on the barracks slackened. Every third day a spoonful of sugar was piled beside our dinner. Even jam and butter appeared. (When this rich food was eaten, however, it resulted in violent stomach upsets for prisoners whose stomachs had lost even a memory of such fare.)

The most apparent effect of the outside world's events was in the release of a few prisoners. They were sent forth as evidence of Soviet goodwill.

Soon it became obvious that the trickle of releases was to broaden into a flood. A small enclosure of wire was strung inside the main camp area to provide a quarantine area for prisoners about to be released. In that area a few lectures and some better food were supposed to erase any hostile memories the prisoners might have. (Some 8000 were under the ground outside our electric fences.)

By mid-1948 about 7000 prisoners had been released. Three thousand, including my father and me, remained. Hope that the remainder also would be released rose suddenly, despite the usual prisoner reluctance to be optimistic about anything. A small force of 200 prisoners was cut away from the main body. Their job, we heard, was to dismantle the camp. It was being closed!

The fact that the camp was being ended did not mean our imprisonment was also ending. We were merely being transferred, and when the location of our new prison was announced, I do not imagine there was a single prisoner brutalized enough to be totally numb to the suggested horror. The new prison was to be Buchenwald.

As we were transferred we could see many airplanes in the sky. They were the planes of the Berlin airlift, shuttling across the skies to bring relief to a beleaguered city. There were no planes to bring relief to the enslaved and imprisoned.

Buchenwald turned out to be a relatively brief part of the prison odyssey. My job there was making sand—by pounding gravel with a carpenter's hammer—and transportation work. There was the same hunger, the same depravity among many of the prisoners, the same hopelessness, the same flarings of brutality, the same deaths and punishments. Buchenwald had been branded as a virtual Nazi abattoir, yet, from prisoners who had been in the camp under *both* the Nazis and the Communists, I heard repeatedly that things were even worse *now*.

It was at Buchenwald, as a matter of fact, that I heard of perhaps the most grossly obscene performance I've ever known. To gratify the lustiest of the women in the camp—and at their request—a cobbler-prisoner had rigged an ample leather phallus to a device built on the frame of a bicycle. The phallus, attached to an eccentric drive, operated through the seat as the "rider" worked the pedals.

On January 15, 1950, a new release of prisoners began at Buchenwald. It was like the last camp and the one before. No one was particularly optimistic. No one was particularly pessimistic. Even my father who, among all the prisoners in Buchenwald, had at least had enough energy left to list his complaints forthrightly when a so-called "medical inspector" had come by, was overcome by general listlessness when it came to releases. It always happened to "the other fellow." It was better to feel that way. Hope, in these prisons, was just something to disturb the stomach and make it churn more around its animal feedings.

Only once, in Buchenwald, did I see the gray of prison routine give way to something brighter. It was when, on two occasions, the prison authorities permitted regular religious services to be held. I say regular, because in the somberness of the prison there were always a few who, with their priests and ministers, held clandestine masses and services whenever possible. Even if they had lost hope in human freedom, they never lost the hope and freedom of interior faith.

But when, at Christmas and Easter, regular services *were* permitted, there was a brief, day-long surge of light even among the prisoners. Women who had grown used to filth and slovenliness cleaned themselves and brushed their hair into a semblance of order. Men to whom mud and odors were part of the dress of every day brushed their ragged clothes and used the water in their wash-

64

CAMP BUCHENWALD

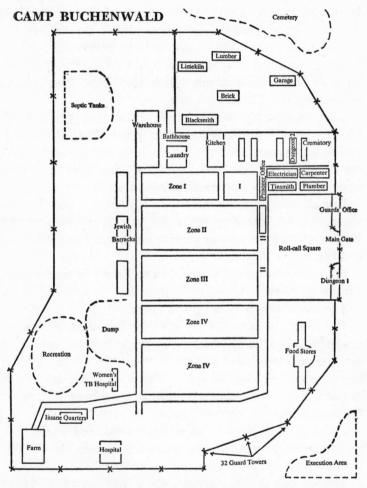

NOTE: The crematory and dungeon 2 were so used until 1945 only. The women's TB hospital was an official house of prostitution until 1945. The execution area was so used until 1945, and the cemetery from 1945 to 1950.

basins for something more than a perfunctory dab at the eyes. Rumors of freedom never did that for these people. Increased rations didn't do it. News of Soviet reversals internationally (which were rare) didn't do it. But the chance to go before their God again in public did it.

The Soviet has always called this a weakness. It is perhaps the only thing about which they have been wrong in judging the Christian world.

Late in January, just as suddenly as they had started, the releases from Buchenwald stopped. Instead, investigating teams went through the ranks of the prisoners, asking questions by rote and "arresting" prisoners for whom some special fates apparently were in store.

I was one of those arrested. My father and I were separated, not knowing whose lot would prove to be the better one. Not for four and a half years was I to learn what had become of him.

Prisoners like myself were taken to Erfurt, some 60 miles from Buchenwald.

The nightmare was unreeling faster.

In Erfurt we were herded into the basement of a large commandeered house. More questions, largely repetitious and meaningless, were put to us. We slept on straw-filled bags tossed on the basement floor. Outside, an organ grinder played the same anguishing tune over and over: "Komm zurück" ("Come back").

From the basement, with a suddenness that could only be terrifying for people who had lived in timeless suspension for so long, we were taken to the prison of Weimar.

In that prison, by contrast, there *was* no time. There almost seemed to be no life. Prisoners stared blankly at the newcomers. No one spoke. In Weimar, as in most prisons, news was tapped from cell to cell. If a person had a question that he wanted answered by a faraway prisoner, he could count on its taking weeks to reach its destination. I heard that there were Americans, British, and Frenchmen here. Who were they? Why were they here? Would they pass along the word of my presence if they were freed?

As long as I was in Weimar I had no answer to these questions. Four years later I was to know their names (William Verdine and Homer Cox were two of the Americans), and one even participated as one of my liberators. Verdine tried to escape from Weimar, after knocking two guards over the head with a pipe. He was caught by the last outpost between him and freedom.

Weimar was, we learned, a prison where sentences were passed. I thought back to the many I had noted as an aide at Münchenerplatz. Now I knew I would go through it firsthand. I tried to minimize it by recalling all the details from the other prison. It didn't help.

The scene, when the day came, was just as I knew it would be, but still shocking in its all-pervading symbolism —Red flags, red drapes, the secret-police officials at the red-covered table. A girl at the table asked the inevitable, routine questions of identity and then shoved a printed form toward me. It had been filled in at two places. First there was my name. Then there was a space with the figure "15" written in.

"What is this?" I asked, pointing to the figure.

"You have been tried in Moscow and sentenced to fifteen years of slave labor." (The paper read: "physical labor.")

It was like being slapped. I could feel the muscles of my stomach begin to give way in a surge of fear.

"Why, for what reason, on what charge?" I blurted out.

"If there are any questions," the girl replied curtly, "ask them where you will be sent." I was shoved from the room.

Back in my cell, I discovered that my blanket and belongings already had been wrapped and thrown onto a stack with the bundles of some forty other prisoners who had been sentenced *within the same hour*.

I had no chance even to try to contact my father or to ask where he was or if he had been sentenced. With the others, I was herded into a big room. We were left there, with only the barest rations and with no word whatsoever, for two days. Then we were packed into police patrol wagons.

Some of the prisoners guessed, from the direction we were following, that we were headed toward Berlin. How right they were came home to us in the cruelest fashion when, at one point, our wagon got lost and drove right to the border of the U.S. Zone. Through slits in the side of the wagon we could see American soldiers at their posts along the street that marked the border. The guard with us in the van enforced silence with his submachine gun, waving it angrily at us as we jammed up to the slits to see the soldiers of the Army of Liberation.

Our stop was Lichtenberg prison. Whereas Weimar prison had been dead with the silence of despair, Lichtenberg was a bedlam of terrible and tortured noises. We were held there one week. Never, during that time (from August 10 to 17), was there a silent moment. We found no rest by night or day.

There was regular torture at Lichtenberg, possibly of new prisoners brought in from the Berlin area; there wasn't much sense left in torturing the other, well-broken-in prisoners. The screams from the torture sessions knifed through the prison at all hours. There were the shouts and loud gibberings of the mad. Madness was always a great factor when there were plenty of new prisoners. Old prisoners were those who had *not* gone mad, who had survived and adjusted to their new, mindless life.

After the seven days of Lichtenberg, I was again hustled from my cell and shoved into a stunned, fearful group of prisoners who, with belongings bundled, were waiting like zombies for the next push into an always unknown terror.

The groups of prisoners, this time, were separated into bunches of twenty and herded into brick corrals in the prison yard. We could see British planes landing at a nearby airport. And then the prison trucks rolled up.

This time we did not go directly to another prison but to a railhead. There, in a line of regular freight cars, were the prison cars that we were to occupy. These rolling jails were disguised as mail cars. Inside, they were partitioned into wire cages that would hold about a dozen prisoners apiece. Each car of cages held about seventy prisoners altogether, with room left over for half a dozen guards. Jammed together, inside the cages, with the stench of a thousand previous prisoners like a greasy fog inside the cars, we began to roll away from the setting sun, into the east.

On August 19 we arrived at Brest-Litovsk and were herded from our mail cars across a plank and into regular prison cars. These were easily recognizable. We had heard about them, often, from drunken guards and from those inevitable inmates of every prison who, in their own way, manage to learn everything there is to know about prison affairs.

The cars were called Stalopinskis, after a former Minister of State Security. The Stalopinski is designed and built for no other purpose than to transport prisoners.

As we walked over the plank into the car, we observed something else even more striking. The Stalopinski was not on the usual European-gauge rails. Its tracks were the characteristic broad gauge of the Soviet Union.

10

THE INTERIOR OF A Stalopinski prison car is very efficiently laid out. It represents one of the few real Soviet contributions to design, inasmuch as Russia's main industrial patterns are copied from those of other nations. The Stalopinski is a Soviet achievement, all Soviet.

Down the length of the car, along one side, runs a narrow corridor through which the prisoners may be herded and through which, later, guards may walk. There are wire cages on the side of the corridor, extending to the far side wall, eight cages to a car. In each cage there are three horizontal wooden shelves about six or seven feet wide apiece, like large tables extending from the wall of the car to the wire of the cage.

On each shelf five prisoners are laid out like sausages on a tray. That makes fifteen prisoners per cage, 120 per car. In the "mail" car, with prisoners standing, only seventy to eighty prisoners could be packed. Getting some fifty extra prisoners per car is a genuine, undisputed accomplishment of communism.

The prisoners were placed on the shelves with feet toward the wall of the car, heads against the wire of the cages. Some lay on their backs, some on their stomachs, depending on how they squirmed when ordered onto the shelf. My position was stomach down. I was jammed between other prisoners, feet hard against the train wall, hands at side, chin against the rough board of the shelf, and eyes staring straight ahead through the wire into the corridor.

There was no way to change positions, to arch one's back, to do anything. Twice a day we were taken out to go to the bathroom. At other times, during the day and night, prisoners who could not hold themselves would whimperingly foul their pants and often also the prisoners next to them. Even in the community of hardship it was difficult for some prisoners not to hate the unfortunates who did this.

We stayed on those shelves for six weeks as the Stalopinskis rolled on, northeastward.

Once in a while, from my spot on the shelf, I could see across the corridor and out of a window of the train for a second when the guards drew the curtain back. After Germany we had rolled through Poland. The land had seemed poor, but it had been tilled and sometimes lovely. After Brest-Litovsk, in the Stalopinski, we were in Russia itself and the landscape changed.

It was like a drop back into another age. Instead of the farm homes of Poland, only shacks and sod huts were visible from the train. Log cabins with burlap window coverings, dust, dirt, rutted roads, farm animals grazing in the mud beside the huts—these were the marks of the Russian landscape.

Our first stop in the Soviet Union was at Orsha, midway between Brest-Litovsk and Moscow. The gates of the cage were opened, the guards herded us out, blinking and wondering, into the sun. No one spoke. No one speculated—we were long past that. We just waited, not moving until prodded and the way pointed out. Only our eyes moved restlessly and furtively as we hunted, not for mere sights, but for some clue as to what would happen next, some secret clue that might prepare us for a sudden blow or a new prison, or even a sudden death.

What we saw from the train stop (it wasn't even a station) was a wooden town of some 25,000 inhabitants. There were no sidewalks. The streets were not cobbled but were just rutted paths between board and log buildings. On several corners of these paths there were manual water pumps. A few electric-line poles near the station were the only reminder that this was a place of our century and not from some past time.

The guards marched us, shuffling, into the streets of the town. Livestock, mostly hogs and goats, crossed in front of us as we went into the town area proper. Carts drawn by small Panya horses rattled along the streets, their drivers hardly bothering to glance at us. Few people in the town, as a matter of fact, seemed to consider us unique enough to favor with more than casual glances. Our clothes, we noticed, were certainly not enough to set townspeople and prisoners apart. We all were ragged together.

At open store fronts (there were no windows), heavy, often barefoot women in padded blouses haggled over bolts of coarse cloth or for pieces of farm hardware. Men in visored skull caps, cotton shirts, and trousers that left a universal gap of inches between pant-bottom and high-shoe top walked about their own business.

There was, we noticed after we had crossed the entire

town, one brick building after all. It was the one toward which we were heading. Just as the Stalopinski is a sign of genuine Soviet progress, so was the lone brick structure of Orsha. It was the prison.

Once through the gates and into the courtyard of the prison, we were greeted by a bedlam of shouts from a balcony where a group of woman prisoners, their skirts lifted, welcomed us with the sort of prison obscenities to which we had become accustomed. This time, though, I was shocked to notice that some of the women, holding their skirts up with one hand, held a child with the other. Women were permitted their children—*and* their excesses —in Soviet prisons as another sign of the enlightenment of communism's penal "kultur."

Our quarters in the prison consisted of a single, hall-like room into which all the Stalopinski passengers were driven. The whitewashed walls were black with a floor-to-ceiling patchwork of names, scratched, penciled, and in a few cases written in blood.

I can remember only one of the names on that wall. I saw it quite accidentally. The name was partially obscured but it was either Roberts, Robertson, or Robinson. By it was a date of just a few days earlier (mid-August 1950), and after it was the identification, "Maj., U.S.A." Here was another far-from-comforting reminder that the power of the Soviet was great enough to snatch other Americans from freedom and into the night of the prison world.

Before the doors were slammed on us, a guard shouted that anyone else caught writing on the walls would be punished. To the packed mob of prisoners, pressed against the walls and filling the hall, the unenforceable nature of the order provided a moment of high humor.

That night the humor was removed when a prisoner, clumsily climbing onto the cooking vat left in a corner as a toilet, toppled the entire vat, spreading its noisome load over the floor on which we had to sleep.

In the morning it was a relief to hear that all prisoners were to get a bath and, astounding news, be shaved! As the long line began to move into the bath and shaving room, however, our joy was qualified. The bathing part consisted of a row of pans. The prisoners shucked their clothes and squatted or stooped over the pans, splashing the water where they thought they needed it most. At irregular intervals the filthy water was changed.

The shaving was as unnerving. A girl barber had been assigned the chore. The prisoners were told not to dress as they moved to her part of the bath and barbering room.

Head hair, she trimmed in seconds, down to the scalp. Then she removed body hair, as expressionlessly as when she was clipping our heads.

Later, from wise prisoners, I learned that this was neither an unstudied vulgarity nor an accident. The Soviet prison authorities had long known that for many men the ordeal of being exposed to a woman under such degrading circumstances was crushing to morale—should there be any random sparks of it left.

When the bathing and barbering were finished, the prisoners were lined up in marching order again and headed back to the cells.

The Stalopinski in which we had come to Orsha had gone on, and we had to wait for a new one. Thus a day's rest was granted.

At that time, in the Soviet Union, every regular train carried one or two Stalopinskis as a matter of course, and the next day we were marched to the tracks. As we waited there, no one even bothered to stare at us, much less at the Stalopinskis when they rolled up in the line of cars. We were thrown onto our shelves in the Stalopinski even as the regular travelers climbed into their cars and sat on the benches.

One thing I noticed now which I had not noticed when we first arrived at the station—perhaps because we had not come with a passenger train such as this—was beggars, literally scores of them, swarming around the train crying for food or rubles.

Our next stop was Moscow, heart city of the Soviet itself. Moscow, like the other cities of the country, was no stranger to trainloads of prisoners.

11

OUR SHIPMENT OF filthy, emaciated prisoners was greeted at Moscow by a brass band.

The band was not for us, but it was right beside the point at the platform where we were unloaded. The band was playing for a group of children returning from a vacation in Switzerland. They seemed very happy as they met the prosperous bureaucrats and military officers who were their parents. But, just as we had been ignored by the ragged people of Orsha, we were ignored by the well-padded folk at the Moscow station.

Even while the band and celebration continued next to us on the platform, we were loaded into prison vans. This time we could not see where we were going. There was no speculation. The idea of being in the capital of the land that had imprisoned us was a stilling thing.

When we alighted from the trucks we were on the outskirts of the city, at the "Red Press" prison, the largest of the transit stops in the busy Soviet jail world. Compared to the Stalopinskis, the quarters were commodious. We were packed into large cells in groups of between forty and fifty apiece. Metal shelves served as beds, but the luxury of being able to turn over on them was a thankful contrast to the prison train. There were two buckets in the cell, exactly similar. One was for a toilet. The other held a weak tea and later the soup and porridge that was our food ration for four days in the prison.

For fifteen minutes each day we were marched onto the roof of the prison and permitted a 15-minute air-and-exercise period inside a wire enclosure. In other such enclosures other groups of prisoners milled, getting their daily tonic. In the section next to us some 300-400 children, seeming to range in age from about eight years to the early teens, took their exercise.

Only in years were they young. Their pinched, thin faces were hard and set. Their eyes were as lusterless as any older prisoner's. Their oaths, if anything, were fouler and more frequent than those of the older prisoners and, in one important respect, they were considerably tougher than their elders in the prison. They cursed, defied, and even spat at the guards with a spirit we had lost long ago. They took their gun-butt beatings better, too, shrieking and yelling rather than whimpering in a lumpy huddle.

Most of them, I learned, were in the prison for "hooliganism," a term that covered everything from theft to assault. (In Dresden prison, I recalled, there had been a 12-year-old boy sentenced for having murdered a Soviet

76

major. That, possibly, had been an act of resistance associated with Red brutality during the occupation. The youngsters on the roof, I thought, were far too practical for such an action. Their crimes, I was sure, were all harshly realistic crimes of profit.)

Some of the young prisoners, or *volke* as they were called, actually had been born in prison camps, where their parents had been confined. Subsequently they had been raised in government homes from which, presumably, they bolted, preferring a life of crime in the streets. Once in the Soviet prison system, however, the volke were treated just as were the older prisoners. They were, for instance, used as slave labor. The entire Kharkov factory for the Fed camera, a Russian copy of the Leica, I learned, was manned by volke.

Thinking now about the volke invariably makes me shudder. But, then, they were just another detail of the nightmare, no more shocking than any other. We were introduced to another level of criminal at the Red Press prison, and it was a much more meaningful introduction than to the volke. These were older criminals. They were called *blatnois,* to distinguish them from the political prisoners such as, until now, had been the only prisoners I had known.

The blatnois, like the volke, were in no particular opposition to the system that had imprisoned them. They would have been in jail, sooner or later, under any system. The fact that they had merely robbed, raped, beaten, or even murdered was an extremely important difference. Unlike us, they were not "untouchable." They were not "degenerate" agents of the Fascists or capitalists. They were not saboteurs, spies, wreckers, counterrevolutionaries or any of the terrible things that we were. They were not,

77

in short, dangerous in any way to the Soviet as such. They were, instead, often helpful.

There was an obvious respect for the blatnois on the part of many of the MVD guards, for instance. The blatnois could be trusted. They could even be called on to assist the guards. The blatnois wouldn't try to escape because, in reality, they had all the comforts and securities *in* prison that they had tried to steal *outside*.

One secret of their success was simply that in many instances they were given carte blanche to run the prisons from the inside. So far as "politicals" were concerned, the blatnois were boss. The guards would turn away while the blatnois beat prisoners. Later I was to see them turn away even from murder. The blatnois stole from the prisoners with impunity. They could force entire shifts of prisoners to work for them. They were, ironically, protected in their crimes by the police!

Because of the special place occupied by the blatnois or common criminals in the Soviet prison system, a few are interposed into most groups of prisoners. The ones sent to join our group in the Red Press prison left no doubts as to their role. In our enclosure inside the jail they flung prisoners away from them to clear a good space for sleeping. When the food was served, they ate first, scooping any scraps of vegetable or solid from the soup or porridge. Only when the blatnois were fully fed did anyone else approach the food tub.

The morning after the blatnois came, the first thefts were noticed. Blankets, shirts, any riches that had been brought from Germany, would disappear as soon as noticed by the blatnois. When a prisoner tried to reclaim a stolen article he faced a brutal beating. Several were beaten before we learned that the blatnois were not to be questioned or disobeyed.

From Red Press we were trucked back to the railway and to the Stalopinski. The blatnois, although they had to lie on shelves like the rest of us, were not packed five to a shelf. Even in the Stalopinski they had special privileges.

We arrived at Vologda, three hundred miles to the north, reputedly the oldest prison in the Soviet, a tower-studded, looming fortress of a place.

We were taken from the train to the prison in trucks. One overturned. The injured from the wreck were shoved into other trucks. A few crumpled bodies were simply left.

At Vologda we were taken to the basement of the building and into a single large cell. These old prison walls had served in the time of Catherine the Great, a harsh ruler in her own day.

We had hardly settled down when the rats started creeping in from all corners. We dared not kill one, for fear the others, smelling blood, might take revenge. All we could do was to share our bread rations with them to keep them from creeping up to us.

We had not been there long when a door swung open and an officer entered and demanded loudly, "Who has had clothing stolen by the blatnois on the way here?"

There was dead silence. Could this be a trap? Were they looking for squealers? I looked around at the blatnois who had been with me and who I knew must have stolen from me. They sat calmly, their eyes fixed on me to see how I would react.

Five or six Germans reported they had been robbed. Before leaving the cell with them, the officer turned to me

79

and said, "How about you, Noble? They took a lot from you too. You'd better come and see what belongs to you."

The bandits had, indeed, taken a good deal from me, but was it worth claiming? I might, in the long run, have to pay a high price for its return.

Before I knew it, I was up and going through the door. We were taken to the office of the commander, where we saw a big pile of clothing. As I entered, I caught a glimpse of the commander leaving through the back door with two of my shirts under his arm.

"Johnny," I said to myself, "you'd better watch your step." If only I could speak and understand their harsh language I could work my way through this jungle of sly crookedness.

I picked up a sweater, underclothing, a coat, and some small articles the blatnois had stolen from me. They were practically all I had had; I had come into possession of them only a short while before I left Buchenwald. They had belonged to men who now were resting in the cold soil outside the camp. Even so, I had more right to them than these crooks had.

I turned, ready to go, when the whole gang of blatnois was led in. We were asked to point out who had stolen from us. When it was my turn to tell, all the blatnois had already been accused by others. I merely said that most of them had been around me in the train, and I could not be sure that it was one or the other.

When we all were back in the cell, I could sense that the robbers were bent on revenge. This was not to come until later.

We were taken back to the railroad tracks and loaded not into Stalopinskis but into regular boxcars. They seemed like luxury coaches by contrast.

But once the doors were slammed shut, the blatnois took over. The dozen blatnois among the seventy prisoners in the car began a thorough search. Everything they had stolen before went back into their possession. No one resisted.

Then the punishment started. At random, the blatnois selected prisoners who had reclaimed stolen goods. I was not, fortunately, among them, since, in their opinion, I had handled myself decently. They merely demanded a sweater from me to prove their authority.

One man who had scrambled onto one of the four sleeping shelves at the end of the boxcar was hauled out by the legs, his head crashing onto the floor, where he was kicked unconscious.

Another man was held up against the wall and beaten unconscious, until his dead weight dragged him to the floor. Then another prisoner was grabbed, stood up in the same place, and beaten until he fell. No one moved. Everyone watched, silent, unprotesting.

At our next toilet stop, four of the beaten prisoners were taken from the train and left, presumably to die from exposure and loss of blood.

The fact that the guards didn't blink an eye at the brutality of the blatnois was warning enough that the return of the stolen goods had been some odd exception, a repetition of which might never occur.

One of the prisoners with us in the boxcar was a Russian-Chinese who was familiar with the course the train was taking. He had been in the Soviet north before—as a free man, not a prisoner.

The man had been in business in Harbin when the Soviet consul there had persuaded him that an outstanding career would be available to him as a plant manager in the glorious Soviet Union. High wages, payment of all expenses, prestige such as few in China could envision were some of the lures proffered. When the Russian-Chinese asked if he could take a piano along for his musically inclined daughter, the consul laughed. Why, everyone knew, he said, that far better pianos, for far less money, could be obtained in the Soviet Union.

The Russian-Chinese was assigned as an official of a chemical plant at the town of Molotov in the Urals. There were, however, a few flaws in the dream world that had been promised. For one thing, his pay was just one third of the promised reward. Instead of luxury and a "people's" piano, he was given a one-room apartment with a kitchen shared by five other families. His daughter, in this new communal environment, was soon sleeping with a notable succession of young Communists. Although the daughter was soon quite contented with the good life in the Soviet, and in the dormitories of the Soviet's young heroes, the father was unhappy. When his time came, theoretically, to choose between staying in the Soviet or returning to Harbin, he chose Harbin. Within a few days he was on his way into the prison circuit.

We also had in our group a woman prisoner. We did not see her, however, after we switched to the boxcar. She traveled with the guards. Sometimes, above the clatter of the train, or during toilet stops, we could hear her as the guards, in shifts, "entertained" her.

During the trip, whenever we stopped on a siding to let another train pass on the single-line track, several guards walked outside the car banging on each board with mallets to assure that none was loose. The hammering was maddening. Once, when we were on a siding for an entire day, the guards kept up the nerve-shattering tattoo almost constantly. It seemed to be fun for them.

On these occasions, when the banging stopped it seemed a great relief. For a time the prisoners would talk, or shuffle their feet, or strain their eyes at cracks in the car wall to see the bleak landscape. After a few minutes, if the train still hadn't started—and stops of several hours were most common—the silence would start. The wind would sigh through the car. No prisoner would have anything else to say. The blatnois would be hunched by themselves. It was then, I suppose, that most of us realized how utterly lost we were. We had only rumor to tell us our destination. We had only our fears to tell us our future in any direction.

There, in the silence of those stops, we realized the most desolate thing that a human can know—that no one cared about us and that no one could do anything about our plight. It was as though the Soviet had made time stand still and paralyzed history itself.

In the silence, once, a man suddenly shrieked and buried his head in his arms, overcome with despair.

The shriek died away. Only the cold Russian wind was left.

During these weeks of travel, the utter monotony was broken every now and then when one of us would see, through a crack, a new prison compound. Some were crowded with men, others with women; some showed no sign of life at all.

As we rolled onward, day after day, the hours of light became fewer and the dense forests faded away. Pine trees had become shrubs; birch trees were thin and spotted. Bushes and grass were sparser.

We arrived at a forest—a forest of poles and barbed wire. It covered part of a plateau which was open only toward the north and northwest, being otherwise surrounded in the distance by the snow-covered peaks and slopes of the Ural mountains. We had penetrated far into the north, beyond the Arctic circle. We were in Vorkuta.

12 WHEN THE ROLL

call at the Vorkuta railroad siding was finished, the Russian NCO barked something like "Shagom marsh!" It sounded like "get going" in any language. We crossed the tracks and walked two abreast toward a small group of buildings, which I later learned was the *peresilka,* the transit camp for new arrivals. The MVD guards with submachine guns and two police dogs took up the rear. Suddenly, a guard shouted an order.

"What did he say?" I asked the man beside me.

"Not to turn our heads or look back or try to break line. If we do we will be shot."

Inside the *peresilka* I was given a two-minute examination by a female doctor and pronounced fit for heavy-duty work. I was issued the slave outfit common to all Russia, a blue cotton-padded jacket (*bushlat*), cotton-padded pants, and a cotton hat (*shapka*) that had flaps for the ears. Across the hat and on the upper right leg of my pants, my slave number, 1-E-241, was sewn on in black cloth. There was little chance to forget who or where I was. From the coded numbers the MVD officials could tell at a glance that I was a political prisoner.

Two weeks later I was put on a train headed still farther north, along with a group that was mainly composed of Russians and Ukrainians. The Russians had been arrested for "treason" or "agitation" or were former Red army men who had been captured by the Germans in World War II, a twenty-year offense. Most Ukrainians were from the nationalist Bandera army that fought the Reds for independence.

We made a short stop at the town of Vorkuta itself, comparatively "modern," with street lamps, cobblestoned roads, planked wooden sidewalks, and bronze statue of Josef Stalin extending greetings to the Komsomol membership, the Young Communists who were supposed to have built the polar town.

In the darkening streets we could see a few hundred slaves like ourselves, their numbers still visible on the cotton clothes in the evening light, with picks and axes repairing streets and breaking ground for a new apartment building for MVD officials.

"Look at the Komsomol'tzy!" my Russian companions laughed.

From the town we went north about twenty miles into the far northern region of the Vorkuta complex. Our destination was Camp 3, where 4500 men worked three of the forty coal pits of Vorkuta. With 120 other men I was assigned to a low, ugly barracks, No. 46, about a mile and a half from Mine 16, where I was to work as a slave for the next three years.

Our barracks were low, rectangular affairs propped just above the tundra. Posts had been jammed into the frozen ground, and boards nailed along them inside and out to create walls. The space between the walls was filled with ashes for insulation, then the walls were covered with mud and straw to fill the holes. When completed, the whole thing was whitewashed.

It was October and the six-week summer was over. There are only two seasons there, summer and winter. A sheet of snow already covered the ground. Prisoners were working outside the barracks, packing the snow into large blocks and propping them up against the side of the barracks, igloo fashion, as protection against the real cold ahead. Within a short time the temperature would drop to 45 to 65 below zero.

I looked at the "bunk" I had been assigned to. It was a segment of a two-foot width of long, hard, wooden shelf, one of two shelves, upper and lower, that ran the full length of both sides of the barracks. I got an upper shelf and shimmied up a pole in front to get there. There was no sheet, mattress, pillow, or blanket—just a hard wooden slab. I untied my roll of extra clothes. Unfolding the trench coat I was wearing the day of my arrest in 1945, I put it underneath me like a mattress.

When the next prisoner lay down, a big Russian peasant who smelled of *machorka,* their crude tobacco made from the stem of the plant, our shoulders were touching. (Later, when new men came in, I had only enough room to sleep on my side flat against the next man.) But I was lucky. Some of the men were sleeping on the floor just as packed as I was.

The only ones who seemed to enjoy the arrangement were the *chorni djhopie,* the dark-complexioned Georgians known as the "black asses," many of whom were homosexuals. To them, our miserably close quarters were an Arctic heaven.

The barracks was dark, with only a small window or two on either side and two naked electric bulbs hanging from the roof. Warmth was provided partly by a mud stove at either end, stoked by a slave whose health had been ruined by the work and the cold. Further heat was generated by the 100 to 125 prisoners who jammed the building. At the far end from me was the drying room, a stinking hole where prisoners back from the mine hung up their unwashed clothes to dry.

It was a human jungle, smelly, overcrowded. Everyone, including the guards, spat large globs openly on the floor. The Russians cursed in one continuous flow. Slaves, guards, Red officials—especially the hard woman prisoners—relied more on cursing than on a regular vocabulary.

There was no toilet in the barracks. A crude outhouse with a hole in the snow was our bathroom. It was about 150 yards from the barracks. The first days I ran like a deer through the deep snow in 20-below-zero weather, then raced back, holding my unbuttoned pants to make it without freezing.

One day I noticed that not everyone went to the outhouse as frequently as I did. I investigated a small crowd that had gathered near the door, which was open just a few inches. A wooden trough made of two planks was stuck through it to the ground below. One prisoner was urinating down the trough and the others were laughing. The smart ones, old hands at Soviet slavery, had devised impromptu plumbing to beat the cold at least part of the time. Some of the crowd were yelling "Da," others "Nyet."

They were betting crude cigarettes of *machorka* wrapped in old copies of *Pravda* whether the urine would freeze before it hit the ground. From November on, it almost always did.

A few days after I arrived I became familiar with the security setup. From what I saw, we were precious cargo indeed. Inside the camp, the MVD guards were unarmed (for fear of being overpowered and having their guns stolen), but Camp 3 was surrounded by a twelve-foot-high barbed-wire fence punctuated with tall towers manned by guards and machine gunners. The towers were connected by telephone and an electric alarm system. A few yards inside the outer fence was a shorter one, three feet high. The snowy area between was designated a prohibited zone, *zapretneye zona,* and lit up all through the night and dark days with powerful arc lights. The guards had orders to shoot on sight anyone seen there. The police dogs, conscientious MVD allies, could scout the entire camp by means of a guide wire strung close to the outer fence.

I was sure Vorkuta was escape proof. During my first week a Pole who had lived in Chicago for some years heard about the "Amerikanitz" and dropped in to say hello. He could handle a simple English conversation. I asked him about the chance for escape.

"Where could you go even if you got out of here?" he said. "It might be possible to get past the fences under cover of a snowstorm, but the tundra, the snow, and the cold defeat everyone. Since I've been here, no one I know of has made it. Actually, you are worth more to the Communists than you imagine. The Komi nomads get 10,000 rubles for every slave brought back. It's more money than they have ever seen. They do a good business.

The Red army also has outposts dug into the tundra, and their planes fly overhead looking for escapees. The only hope is to have the courage of the Colonel."

The Colonel, a former Red army officer, is a Vorkuta legend. According to the story I heard, the Colonel was serving a twenty-five-year sentence for having surrendered his troops to the Nazis during World War II. In 1947, when conditions were said to have been so bad in Vorkuta that survival was almost impossible, the Colonel organized a secret army among the slaves. He succeeded in overpowering and disarming the MVD company guarding his camp. With his slave army now fully armed, he marched to the next camp and after a heavy pitched battle defeated the MVD, again commandeering their rifles and machine guns. The Colonel's army swelled with each camp he liberated, and he carefully made plans to march to the Finnish border, eighteen hundred miles away. It was still summer (revolt is possible only in July and August) and the rabble army made two hundred miles over the tundra before it was intercepted by a motorized MVD unit. Every rebel was either killed in battle or later executed in Vorkuta.

Camp 3, with its 4500 men, was run by the MVD, under the command of Major Tchevchenko (a small, skeletonlike man who hated the cold climate) and his political officer, Captain Buikoff ("bull" in Russian), a tall, stolid, thick-necked officer who threw prisoners into the *bor,* the camp prison-within-a-prison, merely on the word of the *stukachey,* the MVD informers. (The word means "knocker" in Russia, the sign of a coward in a country where no one knocks before he enters a room.) Under Tchevchenko and Buikoff were the prisoner-officials, the *nariaycheks,* in charge of an entire work shift; the

89

desetnicks, in charge of one type of work (e.g., coal mining), and the brigadiers, overlords of anywhere from five to forty men. Ninety-five percent of the camp were violently anti-Communist, but some of the prisoner-officials were still loyal to the Kremlin despite their slavery—and a few served as *stukachey.*

Unofficially, however, Vorkuta had a different master. Our camp was ruled with a steel fist by about 250 blatnois, the Russian criminals. They kept the political prisoners in abject fear. There were about eight of them in my barracks, living on a shelf at the far end that would normally hold more than twenty prisoners. They spent their time sleeping, stealing whatever they admired, sharpening the knives they made, playing homemade balalaikas, dancing the *plashska,* a fast dance something like the Spanish Flamenco.

The bodies of many of the blatnois were covered with grotesque tattoos. I saw one that had the Pope and the Devil in an uncomplimentary pose. Another blatnoi had a giant foot-wide tattoo of human testicles etched in red across his chest.

No brigadier, including my boss, Politayev, a former Red army commissar and *politruk* (political officer) serving a twenty-year sentence because he was captured by the Nazis, would dare ask a blatnoi to work. If one of them should as much as lift a shovel, he would be murdered instantly by his comrades.

The blatnois were unemotional professional criminals, mostly in their twenties, serving comparatively short sentences for theft and murder. They had begun life as *besprisorni,* the vagrant children that travel in small bands throughout the Soviet, robbing as they go. They had been raised under communism, but they knew nothing about politics and cared less. Their *starshi,* or chief, a cold-eyed, burly twenty-three-year-old Moscovite, controlled his men with iron discipline. That discipline was the blatnois' strength over the bickering politicals.

The day I arrived, an Estonian slave had two teeth knocked out and his cheek cut open. He had refused to give his new *bushlat* to a blatnoi in exchange for an old one. One blatnoi did the actual fighting while two helpers stood by. The Estonian made a move toward the blatnoi, but as he did, one of the thief's helpers tripped him. He fell on his face to a chorus of laughs. When he got up to fight again, a blatnoi standing behind him pushed him off balance. As he staggered, he was pummeled ferociously in the face until it was a pudgy mass of crimson. The Estonian's frightened slave friends drifted away from the brutal beating without lifting a finger.

The beating was routine. A few days later, though, I saw that the blatnois stopped at nothing to enforce their will. I had dropped into a nearby barracks to visit my English-speaking Polish friend. While we were talking, a Ukrainian walked from man to man, fear etched in his eyes, whispering an announcement of some kind.

"What did he say?" I asked.

"He says the blatnois are playing cards," he answered with the same trepidation.

"What's so important about their playing cards?"

He looked at me patiently as if I were a child. "Come, you shall see."

We walked toward the far end of the barracks. Five blatnois were seated on stools below the naked electric bulb. Between them was a table improvised from a large

91

board. I stood at a safe distance but close enough to see what was going on. They were playing cards intently, their eyes focused on the dealer's hand.

"It looks like rummy," I said to my Polish friend. "Is that the game?"

"It's something like that, but they play with a forty-card deck, from ace to six. Look how they concentrate without a word or a smile."

"What are the stakes?" I asked. "They must be high."

"Very high," he answered solemnly. "Murder. The low scorer has to kill the man marked for death by the blatnois. It happens every week."

A cautious few like ourselves had gathered near the playing table, but when the blatnois kicked over the board in a sign that the game was over, the small crowd quickly dispersed. I went back to my friend's shelf and watched the drama from there.

A young blond-haired blatnoi about eighteen, the loser, pulled a knife out of his belt and calmly approached the lower shelf of bunks about halfway between me and the place where they had been playing cards. He had a padded jacket in one hand and the knife in the other. Sleeping on the shelf was a well-fed prisoner, one of the cooks in the mess hall.

The blatnoi walked silently, without causing a creak in the old flooring, then leaped at the cook. In one swift professional movement he threw the *bushlat* over the cook's head, held him down with a viselike grip around the neck, then jabbed the long blade to the hilt some twelve times into the victim's chest and stomach.

The cook screeched through the *bushlat*. Dripping blood from his chest, he pushed the blatnoi off him. He got off the shelf and started to run down the barracks

92

aisle toward the door. He got about fifteen feet then collapsed and died in a pool of his own blood.

I had never seen such a killing. Without a word, I walked back to my barracks. Later, I heard the aftermath of the murder. The victim had been decapitated with an ax by two of the blatnois after the killing. Then, following their tradition of "honor," the young killer had carried the cook's head in his hand—its bulging eyes still frozen in an expression of horror—right up to the main gate. He proudly confessed the killing and presented the head to the guard as proof.

The cook had paid the penalty for defying the blatnois. As a cook he was an important part of one blatnoi scheme. When a new prisoner arrived, the blatnois often made a deal—they would "buy" the woolen suit he was arrested in and pay for it with a month's extra ration, a second plate of soup at both meals. The blatnoi chief would take the prisoner down to the cook, introduce him and explain. "This man is to get extra soup every day for thirty days." The now-headless cook had refused to go along with the proposition.

The blatnoi killer was given the usual two-month sentence in the camp prison, not a day of it in the cold cell, a special MVD torture reserved for political prisoners. In return for keeping the politicals cowed, the tattooed criminals had the run of Vorkuta. One of their murder victims was found at least once a week, killed in his sleep in the barracks or face down in the snow, his head opened with a food chopper stolen from the kitchen. Only those blatnois who proved too much for even the MVD were shipped farther north to the Arctic Ocean island of Novaya Zemlya (New Land), from which there is no return.

In 1953, the Soviet government changed the penalty

for murder to death, but still the blatnois never got more than two months in the *bor*.

Fortunately, I had one advantage on my side. As the only American in camp, I soon became a museum piece—treated by my fellow prisoners with special respect and awe. Despite all the anti-American propaganda, the U.S.A. is still the land of magic wonders, at least to the Russians in Vorkuta. One day, an old slave came into my barracks while I was lying down. "Look, look, the Amerikanitz," he said. He was pointing me out to friends who had never seen one.

I decided to take whatever advantage there was in being an American. I would play the lone wolf and keep to myself.

13

MY LIFE IN VORkuta was the closest thing possible to a living death. It was a grueling combination of slow but continuous starvation, exhausting work, killing cold, and abject monotony that destroyed many a healthier man than I.

There was no wasted time in Vorkuta. I went to work producing coal for the Reds the day I got there. The brigadier in charge of surface transportation (hauling coal and slate) at Mine 16 was Politayev, the former Red army political officer who looked me over and picked me for his work brigade. My job was to push a two-ton car full of slate by hand. Some of the others chosen complained that they couldn't handle such heavy work.

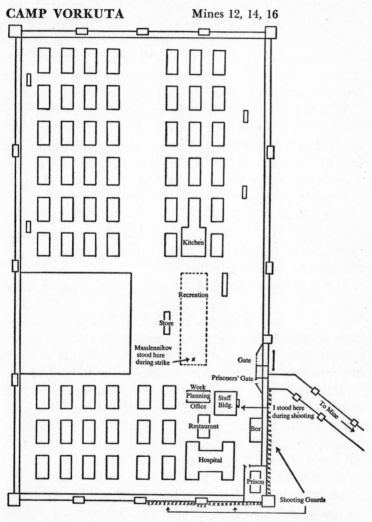

NOTE: The "prison" had 8 cells and was used for severe short terms, in chains, of 5 to 10 days for camp violations. The *bor* was used for confining prisoners serving 10 to 60 days at hard labor for camp violations.

"Sukinsin!" ("Son of a bitch!") one disgruntled prisoner yelled at Politayev. Politayev turned and looked disdainfully at the complaining prisoner. Then he pointed out a slave half-propped up on his bunk. I caught some of the conversation and learned later that he was pointing out a mine slave, one of the unfortunates who worked all day in the 2½-foot-high coal tunnels, crawling on their stomachs and knees like rodents, chipping out the coal. He had a blank, animal-like expression on his face, his hair had turned mostly white, and his eyes were sunk deep in his cadaverous face. All his bones showed under a thin skin covering.

I turned away, sick.

For the next fourteen months, though, my lot wasn't much better than his. In fact, I never expected to live through the winter of 1950-1951.

My day began about 4:45 A.M. when a guard came through yelling "Vstan!" ("Get up!"). The first few weeks I washed with the half of a sheet I had taken from Buchenwald. But one morning when the water buckets froze (a common failure) I noticed that some of the prisoners were washing in the snow stripped to the waist. I decided to give it a try. The entire operation had to be done quickly, I learned by experimenting. One minute was fine, but five minutes could produce a bad frostbite. It stung and my face and body turned a beet red, but I was clean.

"Breakfast" was at 5:30. (The first step out of the barracks each morning suffocated me for a moment, the air was so cold and thin.) There were two meals a day, in the morning and evening. Each morning, I received a pound and three quarters of sticky black bread, which was our basic ration for the day. It was baked less than

96

an hour and soaked with sixty percent of water. It was about one-third the size of an American one-pound rye-bread loaf. It was too wet to eat as it was, so I toasted it over the barracks stove, as the others did.

Breakfast consisted of a scoop of *kasha* (grayish grits) and a small bowl of watery soup with a few cabbage leaves at the bottom. There was nothing to drink except water. Supper, about twelve hours later, was the same kasha and thin soup, plus a thimbleful of sunflower oil to pour over the kasha, a 1¼-inch square of fish, and a roll the size of a small egg. Every ten days, instead of the fish, I got two ounces of tough reindeer meat. Once, on May Day, we had pork.

My whole day's food totaled about 1400 calories (so a Russian doctor told me), about half what an office worker usually requires to live. I was continually starved, my stomach in a knot crying for more. It's a feeling you never get used to.

The evening meal was just enough to engender a real appetite. All I could do to relieve the hunger pains back in the barracks was to brew some homemade "coffee," an art I learned by watching the others. You take an inch-square piece of black Russian bread, stick it on a wire, and toast it over a flame until it is pitch black—but you don't allow it to become white-hot ashes. When it's the right color, you quickly dunk the burnt bread into a cup of hot water until it too turns black. This dirty water is Vorkuta coffee. Strangely enough, on cold nights later on, when I had forgotten the aroma of real coffee, it tasted good.

I had heard about the Vorkuta winter, but I never quite believed it until I saw and felt it.

"It gets bad here in winter," my Polish friend had told

me. "The cold gets in your bones so bad you don't want to live any more. It gets thirty, fifty, even seventy below zero."

I worked on the surface that first year in the worst Vorkuta winter in a decade. After morning mess, I lined up in excruciating thirty-five-below-zero cold, hopping around from one foot to the other while the plodding MVD guards called the roll. My job was a mile and a half away from the camp. Fifty of us, covered by ten guards and two police dogs, made the trip every morning through a forty-foot-wide corridor connecting Mines 12, 14, and 16 with Camp 3. The corridor had the same double set of barbed wire on either side, and the same brilliantly lit prohibited zone. About twenty guard towers were alternately spaced on either side of the corridor. Each tower was manned by one guard, with a submachine gun, who was relieved every three hours.

Winter came quickly. By November and December, the mile-and-a-half trip to and from work took us over an hour each way, as we trudged through snow up to my hips. (The corridor had a wooden walk, visible only in July and August.) Every week the thermometer dipped another five degrees. Within a short time, traveling to work under armed guard became a polar expedition—little Arctic safaris of guards, dogs, and slaves braving below-zero temperatures and blinding snowstorms that blew up out of nowhere. Only the MVD police dogs could forecast them. At the approach of a storm they whined pitifully.

I hit an ugly storm not long after I arrived. It snowed all night, and by morning, the twelve-foot barbed-wire fence on the corridor was only a foot above the snow in some spots. I had never seen anything like it in my life. We ran to the mine through the snow (the pace was killing but it was the only way to create warmth). The snow blew up in front of my face in great swirls. At times the visibility was as low as six inches. The wind howled mercilessly. I was one of the few men wearing the face mask issued by the camp; gradually my breath, captured inside it, began to freeze painfully against my face. I ripped it off and threw it into the snow. I pulled my *bushlat* over my head, and staggered with my arm covering my face.

"Don't break out of line or you will be shot," one of the MVD guards yelled.

I could have stepped right over the buried barbed-wire fence at a dozen spots along the corridor, but there was nowhere to escape to except deeper into the snowstorm.

Suddenly the slave next to me tapped me on the shoulder and pointed to my chin. It was a warning that my chin had turned white, the first frightening sign of frostbite. I pulled my hand out from under my jacket and started to rub the circulation back, the only hope of stopping frostbite. It took ten minutes to get my chin red again. I stopped just in time, for the back of my exposed hand had just begun to show small white spots.

Others weren't as lucky. Hundreds of Vorkuta slaves walked around with toes and fingers missing, amputated after a case of frostbite to stop the gangrene from spreading. One coal miner who had been brought up to the surface on a stretcher after a cave-in had crushed his chest, lay on the ground for fifteen minutes before he was taken to the hospital. His chest finally healed but the short exposure to the cold and snow made it necessary to amputate all his toes and nine fingers.

I never noticed the poor condition of the prisoners until later, when I injured myself and had to go to a dispensary. There I saw how skinny they were. Their pelvic bones were actually protruding through the skin, and from this they were seeking relief; all they got was a new bandage; no extra food, no time off from work.

My own injury consisted of a broken rib and two cracked ribs, suffered during work after I had been at Vorkuta for three weeks. The coal car I had been handling hooked into my jacket and pinned me between the car's sharp corner and a pillar in the corridor where the tracks ran.

Luckily, this occurred at the end of a shift, and I was able soon to leave for the camp. I explained to the doctor what had happened. Because it happened at work, he told me, I must have the mine doctor make a report of the accident. So he gave me a day off to get things settled with the mine.

The next day began one of my monthly three-day rests, and I did not go to the mine until the second day after the accident. The report was made out by the mine doctor, without any trouble, and I went to my department boss to have it countersigned. He said to me: "You had an accident and broke a rib, so you cannot work. How long will it take to get better?"

"Maybe three or four weeks," I replied.

He came close to me and said: "I like you, Amerikanitz, and I want you to work for me, but if I sign this for you, then the next thing I do will be to kick you out. Slave 1-E-241 will work and die in the darkest corner of the mine."

"But why?" I asked. "I didn't break my rib intentionally."

"I know," he replied, "but look: if I sign this, the camp will send you to a place to rest, all right, but I am the department boss and I will have to pay for the time you don't work, and the chief engineer won't get his bonus. You have to confess that you injured yourself intentionally and then take an additional sentence. If you don't do this, you will have to find some way out, but not at my expense. I'll help you along and give you a few days' rest at the mine, and some light work to cover a few weeks, but that's all I can do."

I went off to seek advice on how to close the door that I had opened at the dispensary. My brigadier suggested a second accident, not at the mine but in the camp; I then could say that the first injury was only a sprain but that the camp injury did the real damage. In this way, because the time I lost was not the result of an injury during working hours, the department boss would not be personally responsible for the time I lost from work.

I carried out this suggestion, and so had a day's further rest in the camp and a few at the mine. The chief benefit was that I could stay on the surface and have a boss I could get on with.

When we arrived at Mine 16 on the bitter day that I narrowly escaped frostbite on my chin, there was another roll call. Mishka, a student from Stalingrad, was missing, lost somewhere in the snow corridor. None of the guards volunteered to search for him. The next day, when the storm subsided, his frozen body was found buried face down in the snow. The cold had frozen a pained, lifelike expression in place.

My job at Mine 16 was pushing a two-ton car full of slate. My partner, a Latvian who had done it before, briefed me in sign language on what I was supposed to do. The waste slate dug up with the coal came up the mine elevator and was dumped into metal cars on tracks.

The two of us were supposed to push the car 160 yards by hand, then tilt and unload the slate into another car below our platform. I had to do this seventy times a day, back and forth.

I looked at the tracks covered with snow and the loaded two-ton car. It's impossible, I thought.

Unfortunately, it was only *nearly* impossible, and I became a human locomotive for the next fourteen months. I pushed with my shoulder, jabbing it against the car until my shoulder turned almost permanently blue. Tilting the car was a superhuman strain. The first time I did it, I felt as if my backbone was bending and ready to snap. I never got used to it.

After I dumped the slate, an American-made electric pulley brought it to the top of a sixty-foot-high heap, where it was dumped again.

Every few days I was assigned to work at the top of the heap. The climate sixty feet up was not unlike that on a 15,000-foot Alpine peak. It was horrible. The icy, pricking wind almost hurled me off the slate mountain with every step. It took hours to do the work of minutes.

I worked without protection against the weather. Our tracks were covered overhead with a thin porchlike roof, but we were usually exposed on both sides to the cold, the snow, and the wind. According to GULAG regulations, we weren't supposed to work on the surface in temperatures lower than forty below zero (work went on at all times *in* the mine), but that was a joke. Major Tchevchenko was responsible to MGB General Derevyenko, boss of all Vorkuta, who was in turn responsible to the Kremlin for Vorkuta's coal output. They wouldn't countenance a day's stoppage—even, it was said, if the mustache froze on Stalin's statue in Vorkuta. I worked in

102

fifty and sixty below, my head buried against my shoulder in a pitiful attempt to ward off the cold. One day the thermometer dropped quickly to 72 below Centigrade (—90 Fahrenheit), where it stayed for three hours, freezing the axle grease on my car. But there was still no letup in the work.

More than half the time, we worked in almost inky blackness. During January and February, I worked by starlight at noontime—an eerie experience for one still not used to the Arctic.

I had no gloves, but I managed to steal some oil rags out of the mechanic's shop and wrapped them around my hands. I wrapped my feet in large rags, which were actually warmer than socks. (The Red army uses rags too.) But nothing could keep the cold out. After an hour's work, I was so chilled and exhausted, my face, hands, and feet so numb that I cried like a child.

Officially there was no break in our work, not a minute out for rest or lunch (there was no lunch), but the great institutional Russian inefficiency saved my life. One day, the mine elevator stopped working. There was no slate coming up to us to be pushed in my "baby carriage." A Latvian prisoner pointed across a field to a small building, the mine powerhouse. In a combination of sign language, Russian, German, and English, he explained that it would be about ten minutes before the elevator would be fixed. I raced to the powerhouse, where I was greeted by smiling Russian prisoners warming themselves over a stove. I felt great, except that my boots got wet from the melting snow and they froze when I went out again. From the powerhouse I could hear the signals—two bells for coal, five for slate.

Mechanically, the Soviet mines are very poorly

equipped. This is because of Russia's backwardness, in part, but also because of another factor which the executive engineer explained to me. While Russia has—both on paper and in "show" mines—the most modern machinery, it would not be possible to put this to use generally. Because a modern machine can be operated by one person, replacing from one hundred to two hundred men, this one person is able, if he is "evil-minded" (anti-Communist), to slow down or stop the work of up to two hundred men as represented in the output of the machine. If you have the people themselves to do the work, little harm results if one or two out of a hundred are evil-minded. Why take the risk of using machines?

The mine elevator was a machine they could not replace by man power. Therefore they used the best one available, an American lock hoister built in Iowa in 1913. Almost all electrical machinery was made in America or Germany.

I felt more and more like a primitive slave, my starving body pushing a two-ton car in an age of mechanization. I did not know the language, and I worked all day without a real friend at my side, for they changed partners regularly. I was sure that slaves in other times and places had a better deal than this.

The first seven months of the winter 1950-1951, I had just enough stamina to make it back to the camp every night. After "supper" in the *stolovaya,* our mess hall, I collapsed on my hard shelf in my filthy, snow-soaked work clothes. My face was a deep red from the cold, and for two hours after coming indoors I felt as if a log fire were six inches from my nose. I could hardly lift my stiff legs. My shoulder was blue from the slate car, and the palms of my hands had turned to elephant skin, each palm a large callous insensitive to cold, heat, or pain.

The starvation, climate and work had eaten away my body fat and left me a skin covering that hung over my bones. My weight had dropped to 95 pounds. Where my bones pushed against the skin, the skin turned a deeper brown than the rest of my yellowing but still not bleeding body. My rear end just disappeared. With the fat eaten away, the skin hung in big folds like a toy accordion.

The lack of oxygen in the Vorkuta air complicated my problems. I longed for sleep, but even sleeping all through my day off (three days a month) couldn't shake that all-pervading tiredness.

God, I'm near the end of my rope, I thought to myself desperately one night. If the Reds push me just a little further, I'll break.

The other prisoners were even more wretched looking than I was (although the Russians among us took Vorkuta fatalistically: "What can we do? The regime and I were never friends. The MVD won, so we are here."). They were ill and decrepit far beyond their age. Ninety percent of them suffered from abnormally high blood pressure or heart disease, the blights of the polar region. I had only a slight case of high blood pressure, but my wrists and ankles swelled regularly into puffy masses of skin. Everyone had a cadaverous appearance (average weight was 75-115 pounds), a fact that hit me hard every ten days when we were taken to the camp *banya,* or bath, to get a hot bath and shave and to have our slave's mark of distinction restored—the head shaved down to shiny, hairless scalp. With our clothes off and the filth washed away, the pelvic bones stood out clearly. Only the Baltic prisoners, who received excellent food packages from home when Tchevchenko allowed it, looked any better.

Our teeth rotted from lack of vitamins. There was no dental care—only extractions. Most men had half their teeth missing, especially the lowers. I lost a few, and those I have left are discolored, eaten away, and shaky. Dental problems followed a pattern. The gums around a tooth would start to swell. The expanding fluid inside the flesh gradually pressed against the tooth until it loosened and fell out helplessly—generally while one was eating, especially the leathery reindeer meat served Vorkuta style. Some prisoners frantically tried to stop the inevitable process by puncturing the swelling gums with a needle and draining the fluid.

There was one boon to health. The cold that chilled the life out of us was itself a lifesaver. It was just too cold for most bacteria to live in Vorkuta. Otherwise, epidemics would have destroyed us in a year. Only tuberculosis, probably aggravated by the coal dust, was common.

The heavy labor was almost impossible to avoid. Refusing to work meant time in the cold cell. Prisoners were stripped down to light clothing and put into an unheated stone room, hands chained to the wall, thighs straddled over a concrete block that rubbed the fierce 40- or 50-below cold into the sensitive skin on the inside of the thigh. (Later, a friend, Ivan Simkovich, who had been accused of purposely slowing down his work, was sentenced to five days in the cold cell. "After one night in the cold cell you'll do anything they want," he told me. "It kept preying on my mind. All I wanted to do was get into a warm room.")

No one stood directly over us while we worked, but we had our Communist "norm," more diabolical than any ancient slavemaster. My "norm" was to transport all the slate that came up the mine elevator. Others had more specific tasks—so many feet of shoring in the main shafts, so many tons of coal to be dug, so many feet of coal-car tracks to be laid. Those of us who didn't fulfill their norms were put on punishment rations of less than half the normal diet. It was a vicious cycle. Those too weak to do their work were put on punishment rations. They became weaker and less able to fulfill their norms. The brigadiers, who are always anxious to get the best workers, shunted these poor starving souls from job to job until their emaciated bodies just expired. Those who were fortunate enough might have a sympathetic *feldshar* (one of the half-trained doctors of Vorkuta) declare him fit for only lighter work.

Conditions in the camp hospital were primitive. According to the theory that sick men weren't working and therefore needed less to eat, patients were given only half the normal ration. Only those who had undergone surgery had real beds—the others slept on shelves as we did. But it was still a sought-after haven, a rest from the grueling work and cold.

The hospital was run by a good-looking twenty-year-old girl, called "Doctor." She was actually a *feldshar* with a year of medical-school training. She cursed like a ten-year veteran of Vorkuta, but basically she was pretty nice. Still she had to turn dying men away from the hospital. According to GULAG regulations, only a very small percentage of the work force could be sick on any given day.

A high fever was the only excuse to get in. In the winter of 1950 a group of prisoners transferred to Vorkuta from southern Russia brought in a virus that infected the entire camp within a few days. Only those with 101 Fahrenheit or higher could be excused from work. My fever got quite high, and I spent a welcome week in the hospital. I was given little medication or care, but it was a chance to sleep.

Some slaves who couldn't take the grind dreamed up elaborate escape plans, but these always failed. Three prisoners in a barracks near the fence dug a tunnel from the drying room under the fence to the outside. They made white capes from stolen sheets and skis from old whittled-down boards. They broke out during a snowstorm, but soon lost track of one another. One fell into the hands of a guard at a neighboring camp. Another wandered in a circle for a day and ended up back at Camp 3. The third was found dead in the snow three days later.

Until 1948, escapees were shot immediately. After that, however, they would be thrown into the cold cell—but not before the MVD guards gave them a going over. Since a successful escape would probably mean death for the guards responsible, they beat up everyone who tried, as a warning to the other slaves. I saw one of the three men who broke out on skis. He was lying limp on the floor of the guards' hut at the main gate, his face bloated from constant bashing.

There was really only one way to beat the Communists, and many prisoners used it. That was to disable yourself so badly that you could only be a floor sweeper or the *sushilchik*, the stoker of the barracks stove.

One evening in the middle of the first winter, I was sleeping on my shelf when a loud yell from the end of the barracks startled me. Quickly jerking myself up off the shelf, I saw an Asiatic Russian prisoner, a fierce-looking Kalmuk, one of the remnants of what was once the Kalmuk

Autonomous Soviet Socialist Republic. He had been arrested during World War II resisting the Russian genocide of his entire nation. The Russians killed and imprisoned almost all the 225,000 Kalmuks, including babies and women, and discontinued the "republic" in 1943 when the Kalmuks refused to fight for their Soviet oppressors.

He stood in the center of the aisle. In his left hand was a hatchet he had stolen from the mine. All eyes were on him. He placed his right hand palm down on a stool directly under the naked electric bulb.

"Russki Cherti! [Russian Devils!] No more work from me!" he shrieked at the top of his lungs.

As the words came out, his left hand swung the hatchet down in a resounding blow that struck the hand just above the knuckles, severing his four fingers cleanly from his hand. As he lifted the stump, the blood fountained out and covered his face and clothes. The force of the blow had thrown what once were four fingers onto the floor. His eyes were shining with fierce pride. He wrapped two filthy rags around the remains of his hand to absorb the blood, crawled back onto his shelf, and chanted himself to sleep, cursing the Russians. The Kalmuk spent two months in the camp jail, but he never again did a day's heavy work for the MVD.

Others rubbed dirt into self-inflicted foot or leg wounds and massaged the wounds until they couldn't walk. Some had their friends crush their wrists with six-inch poles. The shrewd ones threw apoplectic fits and tried to simulate high blood pressure by drinking vast amounts of fluids before an examination. Some succeeded, others got time in the cold cell and heavy jail sentences for "sabotage." Tchevchenko blanched and raged with fury at the news of any new self-made cripple. He was deathly afraid the trend would spread and that his wards, Mines 12, 14, and 16, would no longer send enough coal to warm Leningrad.

14

I LIVED IN THIS mad world for more than half a year almost entirely alone, and with little to occupy my mind. Playing cards and singing were strictly forbidden. No more than five men were allowed to congregate at one time. Radio Moscow blared out of the barracks loudspeaker in a foreign language I couldn't speak or write, and which I could hardly understand. As I later found out, there were some women, but I was a Vorkuta greenhorn. Each of the nationalities was organized into something resembling community life, but, besides an odd Canadian, I was the only American in my camp. (I had heard rumors about Private William Marchuk, Private William Verdine, and two other Americans, Homer Cox and Towers, as well as many others, but I had no chance to meet them.)

Days passed into weeks, weeks into months. I wondered whether the U.S. government knew where I was. Were they doing anything? I received no mail or packages (Tchevchenko wouldn't let them through even if they arrived), and I wasn't allowed to write my mother and brother George in Detroit, or my father, who I thought was still in a Russian prison in East Germany (actually he was released in 1952 and was back in Detroit), or the U.S. Embassy in Moscow. They even refused me a Red Cross postcard, a basic international right.

But mostly I thought about food—strangely enough, not about exotic dishes or steaks or ice cream, but plain milk and fruit. I saw shining white glasses of milk and clean pears and apples in my dreams. But I never saw them in reality for nine years.

Sitting on my bunk, I watched some of the other lucky ones get packages from home, for them the difference between life and death. The Russian packages from the rural areas were good evidence of the widespread poverty, generally just a bag of onions, some tea leaves, and dried vegetables. Only rarely they included a small piece of bacon. The Latvians, Lithuanians, and Estonians, whose countries' former prosperity hasn't yet been completely destroyed by Red rule, got full, wholesome packages of candies, sugar, bacon, lard, and sausages. Each package was quickly divided among the prisoner's hungry friends, who tried to make the wonderful gifts last a day or two. Unless it was cleverly hidden, though, food or dried bread might not be husbanded. Molkov, a short, hated MVD guard (unlike most others, easy-going slobs who closed their eyes to most things unless another guard was along), regarded food saved for a hungry day as "evidence" that a slave was making "escape preparations." It was worth six weeks in the *bor* for one of our Lithuanians, Scichkauskas.

My stomach envied those who got packages or who had friends who got packages. I had neither. Then I heard there was a chance to pick up bits of leftover food down at the kitchen after the evening meal. One night, before the evening roll call, when we were locked in for the night, I went to the *stolovaya* and approached one of the well-fed cooks.

"Yeda, yeda" ("Food, food"), I begged in rehearsed Russian. I pointed longingly at the discarded fish heads

111

and a small pile of *kasha,* scrapings off the prisoner-officials' plates. The cook looked me over to see if I was a friend, a friend of a friend, or a quick man with substantial *blat* (bribe money). When he decided he didn't know me from Adam, he kicked me out of the kitchen with a menacing wave of his food chopper. I went back to the barracks a little hungrier, lonely, and more disgruntled than usual.

15

"JOHNNY, EVERY-thing in Vorkuta depends on who you know," Vaska, a Ukrainian in my barracks, told me. "With enough *blat* the guards and brigadiers will give you the right job. There are few Russians that can't be bribed. You need friends in the kitchen for a little extra food, and a contact in the hospital will also never hurt you. If you are part of a tight-knit group, not even the blatnois will bother you." He was right.

Learning Russian was my first survival project. My teacher was a barracks mate, Ivan, a former student at Moscow University, one of the many disgruntled Soviet intellectuals. Without realizing it, I had already picked up a few words on the slate job—"pull," "stop," and others from the guards' commands. In no time I was making excellent progress. "Soon you will speak better than many of the Ukrainians," Ivan said. I worked at it every spare minute, and in a short time could speak halting, grammatically poor Russian.

Now that I was out of my cocoon, my circle of friends

grew rapidly. Three prisoners, Vaska, Ivan, and Alexia, became my closest friends. Vaska, a twenty-five-year-old, short, dark-haired Ukrainian peasant, worked the electro-pulley that hauled my slate to the top of the heap. A fervent Ukrainian nationalist, Vaska fought with the Ukrainian Banders army during World War II against both the Nazis and Communists. Ivan, a thirty-year-old Ukrainian, had some secondary education—somewhat of a rarity in the rural areas. He hated the Communists with a passion reserved for Ukrainians. Three million of his people died of famine in 1932 during the severe drought. Red troops closed the Russian-Ukrainian border to keep the starving people from leaving, and stole whatever grain existed. Both Ivan's parents had been deported to Siberia.

"Millions were sent to Siberia or killed in the 'thirties when the Communists forced us to collectivize our farms," another Ukrainian told me. "When Hitler invaded Russia it was a chance to fight back against the Kremlin. We had millions of soldiers ready to destroy Stalin. But when we saw that Hitler was no better—he kidnaped thousands of our people to work in his factories and had no intention of giving us independence—we had to fight on both fronts. We died on the west against the Nazis and on the east against the Communists. It was hopeless."

Alexia was a Russian from Smolensk. He had been arrested in 1946 while a senior high school student, charged with the ubiquitous Paragraph 58-10, Agitation, the standard charge for anything from telling jokes about Stalin to intellectual deviationism.

My new friends made life a little more bearable. I shared in their meager food packages sent from home. Sometimes a friend in the kitchen could find a little extra cabbage soup or fat to help protect my 95 pounds against the cold. When

113

I went to the camp hospital later, my friends brought me bread saved from their own rations, and other favors for which I'll always be grateful.

Learning Russian dispelled another fear. The language is so harsh I always thought everyone was screaming at me. Later I realized it was just a way of speaking. Actually the Russians are far from firm. They are masters of bluff—but when you stand up to them aggressively, they invariably back down.

Through my triumvirate and my new command of the language, I came to know the more than one hundred other slaves in my barracks, and others throughout Vorkuta. Vorkuta was a veritable League of Nations, and it contained many notables of the Communist world. The former First Secretary of the Communist Party of Estonia, who had labored to turn his country over to the Soviet, was handing out food in the *stolovaya* of Mine 29.

There were slaves who had been deputy ministers of East Germany and satellite countries, and regional leaders of the Communist Party itself. Gureyvich, a Russian Jew and former Soviet diplomat, was in Camp 3 just a few barracks from me. He had been recalled from France by the Kremlin shortly after World War II (when the "cold war" policy developed) and arrested by MVD agents as he stepped off the plane in Moscow. We had a colleague of Trotsky, who had been in dozens of slave camps for the last nineteen years; a former Professor of History at the University of Leningrad, and many former university students. A barracks mate, Dmitri Bespalo, an active member of the Young Communist League (Komsomol) at the University of Kiev, was serving fifteen years for "agitation."

We had many former CP members from East Germany,

who were arrested in periodic purges from 1946 to 1950. There were even two Spanish Communists who had been in Odessa in the thirties expediting war materials to the Spanish Loyalists during the Civil War. They stayed on in Russia after Franco won, and a year later were arrested for "espionage." Most of the ex-Communists were disillusioned with what they consider the Kremlin's perversion of Marxism.

Not everyone in Vorkuta was an ex-Red. We were a polyglot army of slaves from every walk of life and almost every nation in the world. In Camp 3 we had Poles who had served with the Allies in General Anders's army during World War II and were arrested back in Poland when the Communists took full control in 1947. There were hundreds of Baltic people—Lithuanians, Latvians and Estonians, whose nations had been gobbled up in 1940 and made into Soviet republics.

"When the Russians realized they couldn't really communize us," a Latvian, a former resident of Riga, told me, "they started to bring hundreds of thousands of Russians in to live in our country. They sent our people in exile to Siberia. Those of us who fought the deportation are here in Vorkuta, or in Karaganda or Irkutsk, or other slave camps instead of living in collectives in Siberia. Well, maybe there isn't much difference anyway."

Another Latvian had been a student at the University of Riga before his arrest. A prominent athlete, he had often visited Moscow with various sports groups. He confided to me that a good part of the Russian Olympic teams are actually made up of closely guarded, blond-haired anti-Communist athletes from the Baltic nations.

There were slaves from Iraq, Iran, Italy, Mongolia, China, and Czechoslovakia and later two North Koreans

115

accused of disloyalty to their regime. There were a number of Russian and Ukrainian Jews, victims of Stalin's anti-Semitic pogroms of 1949-1953. In Camp 3 alone there were ten Greeks who had been taken prisoner by the Communists during their civil war. One of my barracks mates was a young Hungarian, James, a former university student in Budapest. He had been arrested as a "Western agent," allegedly for spreading Colorado potato bugs, thus causing the bad potato crop in Hungary. There were hundreds of Germans, both Communists and Nazis, and some former SS troopers. We had representation from France in one prisoner, René (his wife was in the women's compound), who had been attached to the French government unit in West Berlin; an Englishman named Chapman (in Camp 10), a British army man who had been captured by the Germans in Holland. He was liberated in 1945 by the Russians from a Nazi PW camp, then promptly rearrested by the Reds and sent to Vorkuta. When I met him in mid-1954, his mind had been almost completely destroyed. Eve Robinson, a good-looking blonde Englishwoman, about thirty, was in the women's camp.

A number of my fellow prisoners were clergymen, Catholic priests from Lithuania, Protestant ministers from Latvia and Germany, and Russian Orthodox priests who were the only ones allowed to keep their long beards. Religion was one of the most serious crimes in Vorkuta. Possession of a Bible meant at least a month in jail.

But, despite all controls, religion flourished. Some groups held services at an altar in an unused hallway of the mine. A group of Baptists sat together at the evening meal in the *stolovaya* and prayed. When an MVD guard came over, they said: "There is nothing wrong, *Chort* [devil]. We are just praying." (The guards in Vorkuta took the slaves' imprecations philosophically.)

On free days I sometimes attended Protestant services given by a Latvian minister. It was in a different barracks each time. It was dangerous, but only if two or more guards came along. Individual guards made believe they saw nothing and walked away. A Lithuanian priest in my barracks was arrested regularly. But after two months in the *bor*, he would return each time to minister to his flock.

I was the only American in Camp 3, but I had contact with a few men who claimed to be Americans. In Camp 10, where I lived in 1953 and 1954, there was a William Vlasilefsky, an English-speaking, Russian-born prisoner who claimed to be an American citizen. He said that he lived most of his early life in the Western states and that part of his family was still living in Seattle. According to Vlasilefsky, he was in the United States army in the early thirties, then migrated to China, where he started a successful business. In 1949, the Chinese Reds called him to Peiping, where he was arrested and sent to the Soviet as a slave laborer.

Then there was Roy Linder, in Vorkuta called Adolf Eichenbaum, a prominent Vorkuta citizen. I met him in the hospital in 1950. Later he would come over to my barracks once in a while to talk. He spoke perfect English and, for that matter, equally good Russian, German, Swedish, and Chinese. We reminisced about Detroit (he had been a stunt flier at the Michigan State Fair) and about the States in general. Linder was very tall and balding and had a scarred chin that was twisted to one side, the result, he said, of a plane crash. According to his story, he was born in Vancouver, British Columbia, was an American citizen and a colonel in the United States Air Force, one of our commanding officers at Templehof Airport in West Berlin. During World War II he had been a U.S. army pilot in China, and prior to the war had flown as a "neutral" observer in the Spanish war.

According to Linder's version of his arrest, he had been kidnaped by the Communists in West Berlin in 1949 and dragged over to the eastern sector. After a year in Lubianka prison in Moscow, he had been shipped to Vorkuta as a slave laborer.

His story seemed convincing (except for occasional references to himself as major instead of colonel), but his short sentence of five years for Paragraph 58-6, "Espionage," made everyone suspicious. An American officer (unless he was trusted by the MVD) would undoubtedly have been tagged with a fifteen-to-twenty-five-year sentence. He had a local reputation as a person who might be pro-Communist. He seemed to have more freedom of action than the other slaves, more to eat, and more respect from the guards and MVD officers. My friends warned me not to trust him—that he was probably an MVD *stuckachey*—an informer.

"Don't worry, Johnny. I won't make any trouble for you," Linder once told me in an unguarded moment.

The last time I saw Linder was just before he was released by pardon. He sent me a note a few weeks later, saying that he was in Vorkuta working in the village powerhouse as a free worker. He had a girl friend in Rostov in South Russia and hoped to go and meet her. I have no idea whether he was ever allowed to leave the Vorkuta area, or what has since become of him.

Many other Americans are still in the Soviet, working as slave laborers. I heard that an American engineer, seized while working for the Reds in Vladivostok, is still in Lubianka prison in Moscow. According to newly arrived slaves coming from Moscow, so is Stalin's son, Lt. Gen. Vassily Stalin. But a Yugoslav who had been imprisoned only a hundred miles from Vorkuta told me more startling news.

"I spoke with eight of your countrymen," the Yugoslav told me. "They said they were American fliers who had been shot down by the Russians over the Baltic Sea. The Air Force has, of course, acknowledged that several B-29s and B-50s on routine missions were downed over the Baltic. One of them told me he was afraid they would never get back to America. The Russians had reported them dead, saying there were no survivors of the crash."

Prisoners being funneled into Vorkuta from camps in Tadzhik and Irkutsk in Soviet Asia, Omsk in Siberia, and Magadan in the Far East said there were many Americans, including veterans of the Korean War, both GIs and officers, and South Korean soldiers, working as slave laborers in their camps. From what I heard, they were PWs captured by the Communist Chinese and North Koreans who had been shipped to the Soviet for safe-keeping.

Some of the Ukrainians in our camp literally fell over every newcomer, questioning him on what prison camp he had come from and how many prisoners were there. Through adding, cross-checking, and striking averages, it was possible to establish a fair approximation to the number of people interned in Russia. The total population of the Vorkuta complex lay between four and five hundred thousand working in mines, brick factories, power plants, railroad lines, streets, city and village construction, food transportation, prison help, and hospitals. According to records we were able to piece together, throughout the entire Soviet Union in mid-1954 a total of twenty-five to twenty-eight million people were held in slave-labor camps, concentration camps, secret camps for foreigners, PW camps, repatriation camps, MVD prisons, investigation centers, MGB prisons, juvenile labor camps, and juvenile detention homes. An additional twelve million not in custody were interned in restricted areas. All told, a monstrous mass of slaves and persecuted peoples.

16

KNOWN THROUGHout much of Vorkuta simply as the "Amerikanitz," day and night I was pounded by my fellow prisoners with questions. How does a worker live in America? How long does he have to work for a suit? It was a generally prevalent opinion that America is the wealthiest country in the world. One of our civilian Communist department managers, a native of the Komi Republic, told me his people lived solely off American canned food during World War II. Most of the shoes still worn in the area came from American war relief.

The Russians themselves admit the superiority. The first few months I was in Vorkuta, a large cloth banner that hung near our mine said: "Follow the example of American technic" (technology). Another Red poster, which may still be hanging in Vorkuta, exhorted the slaves to "approach, reach, and pass capitalist production." Even in Soviet propaganda films, Americans are pictured as better dressed than any Russian I ever met.

I answered questions about America day and night, but

I doubt that they believed more than ten percent of what I told them. My wretched fellow slaves couldn't even imagine a world such as I pictured—until years later, after my almost daily descriptions.

"Johnny," Alexia once told me incredulously, "you would have us believe American workers drive their own cars."

Ivan and Vaska had been Vorkuta slaves since 1946. They were two of the few who survived the horrible early days. Vorkuta's rich coal fields were discovered in 1936, but they weren't exploited until 1942, when the Germans captured the rich Donbas coal region. The first mine was opened by slave labor in 1944, and by 1946 the Russians were expanding the area rapidly.

Ivan told me about it. "They drove us by truck up to this northern region of Vorkuta. There was nothing up there then, just the freezing open tundra. They left us the truck, gasoline, a few guards and some food. 'This is your life,' the Reds told us, 'make of it what you can.' Only the Russians could have such nerve. Wood from the Vorkuta sawmill was transported to our isolated outpost. The first thing we were forced to build was a fence to enclose ourselves.

"We lived in the open for over a month—in wood-lined holes dug in the ground and in tents. We lived off American canned food. Only after the fence was done, did they let us build regular barracks. More than half the men died of exposure and overwork."

During 1947 and 1948, the death rate was unbelievable, Vaska told me. "You are lucky to be here now. You have a chance to live. Things are much more civilized."

I didn't feel very civilized. Despite a small improvement, I was starving. One day, one of my new barracks mates, a

121

Hungarian doctor (and ex-wrestler) came over to my shelf.

"Johnny, did you ever eat a dog?" he asked.

Normally, the thought would sicken me. But the last meat I had eaten was a two-inch piece of tough reindeer meat two weeks before.

"How does it taste?" I asked greedily.

"Very tender and tasty—especially when it's roasted."

That night at work we went dog hunting. The dogs of the guards, and other dogs from the nearby *posiyolok,* the settlements of the "free people," sometimes wandered into our camp. I went equipped with a thick stick and a stolen kitchen knife in my pocket. We waited near the main mine shaft. Suddenly the doctor spotted a dog chasing around the office building. He beckoned to him. As the dog approached us, I swiftly brought the thick pole down on his skull with all my strength. He fell into the snow, unconscious.

"Give me your knife, Johnny."

The doctor cut him open deftly as if he were performing an extensive surgery. We let the blood run out on the snow. We cut the body up into pieces and roasted it on top of my sixty-foot slate heap. When the top pieces of slate were pulled back in places, a natural phosphorus in the mine waste started a spontaneous fire, perfect for roasting meat. We had a hearty meal, then hid the remaining pieces two feet under the snow (a natural deep freeze that could preserve meat for a hundred years) at the four corners of the mine office building.

The doctor was right. Dog meat, I found, has a taste all its own, but if anything, it is softer and tastier than beef. In all, the doctor and I ate up two dogs. The pieces, kept hidden in the snow, fed us for months.

17 THE DOCTOR WAS

a very resourceful slave and a valuable friend. We slaves were at the mercy of the blatnois and the Red officials, but the doctor was not. His weapon was a supposedly powerful sex potion. The frigid polar weather tremendously reduced the sex drive of the men in Vorkuta—slaves and officials alike. For some, like myself, it was a blessing. It was one less misery. But for the civilian mine officials with wives and girl friends, and those who had access to prostitutes, it seemed worse than death.

The doctor came to the rescue. From Georgian prisoners who wrote their relatives, he got hold of a type of cactus, which arrived packed in honey. From the plant, he made a drug that he sold in a series of fifteen injections for as much as 300 rubles. His customers, including the chief engineer of Mine 16, swore that it was an aphrodisiac supreme, but I personally never believed it had anything but money-making powers.

I sometimes helped the doctor give the shots (he once had ten series going simultaneously), and he rewarded me with a rabbit, which I cooked in the powerhouse and devoured.

Sex was openly for sale in Vorkuta to those who could afford it. For the 4500 men in Camp 3, there were ten women, all "free people." They worked the mine ventilators on the surface, switching them off and on, depending on the amount of coal gas in the air. Their lot was not much better than ours. Many of them were former woman prisoners, who now lived in exile in the little settlement near the camp. They earned 400 rubles a month, which wasn't enough to live on. For extra money they turned to prostitution. The standard fee was twenty-five rubles. Only two of the women were attractive. The rest were typically Russian, built like trucks. Some of them were tattooed like the blatnois and they all cursed with a vengeance that put us to shame. But it didn't seem to hurt their business.

The first years, when we had no money, the prostitutes were a luxury of the prisoner-officials, blatnois, and free people. In addition to the girl's fee, an equal amount of *blat* was required to buy off the guard.

An experienced fellow prisoner explained the system to me. "The meeting place is behind the big fan of the mine ventilator. There is a platform there which is one of the warm places in the mine. If a guard who is not bribed should come along, the customer climbs up to the roof of the ventilator building through a trap door, and the girl explains that she was sweeping out behind the fan."

My biggest fear after the first year of pushing the slate car was being forced to work down in the mine. I was half destroyed by working in the cold, but I had also spent one frightening day below watching the animal-like slaves mining coal.

In June 1951 a mining commission arrived from Moscow to study coal production in Vorkuta.

The result was an announcement that the strongest prisoners (that included me) were to work *below* in the mines. I was to be transferred the next week. Quickly I went to

124

see the department manager of transportation, a young Communist civilian employee of the MVD.

"What can I do for you, Amerikanitz?" he asked.

"I'm being sent below. I wonder if I could also do transportation work down in the mine. It would be better than digging coal."

"Anything would be better than that," he laughed. "I'll see what I can do."

I'll never know for sure, but probably because I was an American—and as such, a minor Vorkuta VIP—he transferred me to mine transportation. My job was coupling coal cars and guiding the small trains through the narrow mine shafts.

Vorkuta Mine 16 was a precarious, primitive hole. With little modern equipment and no conception of safety, we had cave-ins almost every week in which one or more slaves were killed or injured. The ceilings of the mine tunnels often collapsed because the wooden posts that shored up the ceiling were spaced too far apart. The department managers saved the wood that was provided for shoring and sold it to the Komi nomads, pocketing the cash. Another scheme was to show a saving of so many feet of wood on their monthly reports and receive a government bonus.

The slaves who did the propping didn't care. Wider spacing meant less work and, since they covered a greater distance, a better "norm." Their safety was secondary to fulfilling the "norm" and getting a plate of soup to eat the next night.

One time, twenty-four men were killed because of primitive equipment. We had no spools for electric cable. It had to be transported through the mine on the shoulders of two dozen of the strongest men. The cable was coated on the outside with tin. The coating at one point was defective. The men were soaking wet from water that dripped from the thawing ice on the ceiling. The result was the instantaneous electrocution of all twenty-four men.

My work was in the narrow mine tunnels that connected the coal faces. The air in the hallway smelled sweet, like rotted mushrooms. When I licked my lips, I tasted gas. Smoking was prohibited, but the *machorka* hounds smoked anywhere. As a result, we had frequent flash fires that lit up the mine like day. The water dripped from the ceiling constantly. By the end of a day's work, I was soaked through. As I hurried home through the forty- and fifty-below-zero weather, my clothes froze into an icy board.

Each morning I brought a piece of bread with me for my lunch. It was stuffed next to my body under my shirt. When I was ready to eat it, it was soaked like a sponge with water and perspiration, smelling of gas, and black from coal soot—but food always tastes good to a starving man. After eating the bread, I cupped my hands and drank the water that dripped from the ceiling. It was prohibited as being polluted, but it was refreshing.

The hallways were six feet wide at the base, and tapered to about four feet at the ceiling. The coal-car tracks took up most of the width except for a foot-wide wooden trough for the falling water that ran along the edge of the tunnel. When a coal car passed, I had to jump to keep from being crushed. Where the hallway was wide enough, I could press snugly against the wall between two pieces of shoring and watch the car pass within inches of my chest. Usually, though, I had to dive face-first into the wooden trough, my body kept as much out of the water as possible by elbows and knees.

126

My brigadier, a Russian German from the Volga Basin, explained my duties.

"We have no automatic switches here, Amerikanitz," he said. "You have to set up the coal trains by coupling the cars, then ride up front and throw the switches yourself."

He made it sound simple. Actually, as I found out, I had to make up physically what the Russians lacked in modern equipment. I rode at the head of a long train of small coal cars. I stood on the bumper, the searchlight on my pressed cardboard helmet trained on the dark tracks ahead. There were no lights other than my searchlight. I scanned the tracks as carefully as possible for open switches. The switches were placed at random all over this catacomb network of coal tracks. When I saw an open switch in time, about five or six feet ahead, I jumped off the bumper, threw the switch, then raced for cover against the wall before the train ran me over. A few moments later, I waved down the engineer of the locomotive thirty cars back. He stopped and picked me up.

Sometimes I couldn't make the switch in time. The first time this happened, I had been bobbing my head up and down to let the searchlight dance all over the tracks. I knew one of the switches was somewhere directly ahead, but I didn't know exactly where. Then, suddenly, my headlamp froze in place just three feet ahead of the train. It was a switch, wide open. There wasn't enough time to close it, so I jumped off the train, pushed desperately against the mine wall beside a shoring post, and waited for the crash. When the coal train hit the open switch, it tumbled off the tracks and piled up in a mass of cars and spilt coal. One of the cars fell right across the shoring protecting me, coming to rest only inches from my chest. If it had fallen just a little in the other direction, the point of the car would have pierced my chest.

These crashes became a regular part of my job. Once, a car split a shoring and brought down a portion of the ceiling. I was bruised badly by the falling stones.

The mine was poorly maintained. One day, after throwing a switch, I noticed that the steel "feather" that connects the two otherwise disconnected rails hadn't closed properly. I rushed out from my alcove refuge and held the feather with my hand until the front wheels caught. It was a risky move. I pulled my hand back quickly. In another instant my fingers would have been crushed by the wheel. As the back wheel approached the faulty switch, I held the feather again until the wheels caught, but when I pulled back this time, my mitten was caught in the switch! I yanked my hand out of the glove just as the wheel rolled over it.

I repeated this little game of split-second timing sixty times, for all thirty cars. There was no alternative. If I missed once, the train would have jumped the tracks and crushed me to death. I got a strange reception when I asked my brigadier to report the faulty switch to the department manager.

"Leave well enough alone, Amerikanitz," he said. "I'll tell him what you said, and you'll end up digging coal like an animal, on your hands and knees. Do what you can with the switch. The officials don't want to hear about your trouble."

My switchman's version of Russian roulette started to disturb me greatly after a while. I longed to get out of the mine. It was in February 1953 that my new department manager, Chumboritsa, a Communist Party member from

128

Georgia, made the dream come true. I had spoken to him once or twice about America, and he remembered me.

"Amerikanitz, how would you like to work upstairs for a change?" Chumboritsa asked one day. "There's an opening in the officials' washroom."

It was the nicest question anyone had asked me in seven years. I started working in the washroom the next day as an attendant. It was a new world.

18

I WORKED TWENTY-four hours on and twenty-four off—my first chance for real rest in years. I slept through my days off for the first month or so, and gradually the constant fatigue of the Vorkuta sleeping sickness began to leave me. The washroom was the cleanest and warmest room in the mine. I had a place to wash and dry out my clothes, and soon I became a sartorial wonder for a slave laborer. The washroom was next to the mine office, and the young Communist executives would change their good clothes in the washroom and leave them with me. On the night shift, they would often come in just to keep warm.

For me it was a university education in Soviet life. There are three kinds of "free people" in Vorkuta; they are the Red executives, actually civilian employees of the MVD, who have been assigned there; workers from all the Soviet Union, who have come to Vorkuta for the "long ruble," the Arctic bonus pay; and former slaves who have completed their sentence and are now in lifelong exile.

There were fifty "free people" in Mine 16—forty workers and ten Communist executives: the chief engineer, his assistants, department managers, and chief mechanics.

I washed out their shirts, gave them towels and soap for their showers or bath, and generally made myself useful. They were genuinely intrigued at my being an American, but at first they tried hard to keep our relationship stiff and formal; I was only slave 1-E-241. But the temptation to discuss America was too much for them, and in a few months we were all good friends—sitting in the washroom talking through much of the cold nights. Often, when they bought some delicacy—like a piece of real cheese—they would bring the leftovers to me. It was all very wonderful.

The average free worker, other than an executive, I found, is completely dissatisfied not only with Vorkuta but with the Soviet Union. The ones I met weren't politically sophisticated enough to discuss communism or capitalism, but they knew concretely that they just didn't make enough money. They lived in one of the four villages or thirty *posiyoloks,* dreary little settlements with a store and a row of one-story barracks-like buildings in the shadow of the coal mines. Each family had one room and shared a communal kitchen.

"I make eight hundred rubles a month," one of the mechanics told me. "I have figured it takes at least 1500 rubles for two to live at all. My wife works in Vorkuta too, for 600 rubles, but it's still not enough." Another free worker only made 450 rubles in our mine. The "long ruble" these people were seeking at Vorkuta was long, but not long enough to reach from payday to payday. Yet, had they been working in any other area—excepting a few capital cities and propaganda mines—their ruble would have been exactly half as long as it was here in Vorkuta.

For the average "free worker" in Vorkuta, clothes were prohibitively priced. The ruble is worth twenty-five cents at the official rate, but it is actually about one fourth that in purchasing power.

From my Communist washroom companions, I learned that the situation is much the same all over the Soviet Union. Except for executives, Stakhanovites (high "norm"), and highly skilled workers, it is a nation of families living in one-room apartments, existing on substandard salaries. The Kremlin for several decades has been siphoning off the profits of Socialist industry for heavy industrial expansion and armament production. The singular exceptions are the large cities like Leningrad and Moscow, where workers get as high as double pay, although they too live one family to a room. Red leaders vividly remember that their own revolution started in the large industrial cities. They have no intention of having history so painfully repeat itself.

There is a tremendous disparity of pay in the worker's paradise. The director of our mine group, Bulbenkov, was paid 35,000 rubles a month—500 times more than the average worker. He and his wife paraded in heavy fur coats and caps and drove a horse and buggy, a great luxury in Vorkuta. Bulbenkov called himself a "true Communist."

My greatest washroom pleasure was arguing with the young department managers, all graduates of Soviet technical schools, members of the Komsomol (Young Communist League), and now members of the Party itself. They are the élite of the Soviet.

131

Like all Russians, they have heard strong rumors about prosperity in America, but are completely confused after reading their government's propaganda about Wall Street and the starving workers. As the ice between us broke, they felt me out carefully.

"Amerikanitz, tell me about how rich your American workers are," one of the young department managers asked me, laughing, but with little enthusiasm.

Each time I described economic conditions in America, I could see their eyes open like those of awed school children. My comments verified the rumors they themselves had heard from Russians who had contact with the West, mostly in Germany after World War II. Their curiosity was insatiable. "How much do shoes cost? Can a poor boy go to college? Do workers actually drive cars? Do you have television in the United States?"

"Well, you may have prosperity there, but it's only a bubble that will burst," one of the seven department managers told me half-heartedly. "When we get prosperity in the Soviet it will be forever. It may not be for five generations, but then it will be permanent. Perhaps it is not so good here, but *budit, budit,* it will be, it will be."

Budit is a key Russian word. Actually, those who haven't already become cynics waiting for the Communist Utopia to arrive try to hypnotize themselves. When I asked: "What about life in Russia, meanwhile?", they shrugged. "That is true. It is sometimes very hard for some people."

These seven young men typify Russia's future. They have the most to gain from communism, but I would say that at least three of them (at the age of 23 to 25) are already cynics. Their pay is presumably excellent, about 3,500-4,500 rubles per month, about equal in purchasing power to that of an average American worker. But they too were dissatisfied. One third of their pay went for income taxes, and one of them told me their compulsory social contributions—for Party dues, youth fees, and other purposes—equaled 800 rubles per month! Room and laundry were cheap, about 50 rubles a month, but after food, clothing, and vodka (at 50 rubles a bottle) they had nothing left.

One of the young men, Shuisky, a native of the Komi Republic, was a prominent Communist, a member of the Town Senate of Vorkuta. One day he came running into the washroom to tell me he was getting married. "Now my wife and I will have a room for ourselves," he boasted. "It will be much better than living the way I am now, with two other men in one room." His "furniture" was being made from rough lumber by a few of the slave workers as an extra job.

The Communists openly admitted to me that there is little freedom in the Soviet. The freedom they missed most, personally, was the opportunity to quit a job and take another. They hated their assignment in Vorkuta and looked longingly at photos of Moscow and sunny southern Russia in *Soviet Union* and other magazines. Some of them half-heartedly defended the lack of freedom. "Our government has a job to do. It could not control the people if they had freedom."

Except for one man, they were far from being Communist fanatics. The Party was strictly a means to a career for them. Few had any idealistic concern with communism. "Of the four and a half million Party members," one estimated, "I would say only five hundred thousand have any interest in world revolution."

While I was in that washroom, I played heavily on their

doubts about life in the Soviet—doubts that were also strengthened by foreign radio broadcasts. The average Russian three-tube set that is openly for sale doesn't have enough range to reach the Voice of America, BBC, Radio Free Europe, or the West German stations. But the department managers, as trusted personnel, could and did buy short-wave radios. There is no Soviet law against listening to such programs as far as I know. A number of them confided to me that they often tuned in the West. I would say it is fairly effective despite its limited audience.

One thing they still wouldn't believe, no matter how much I talked, was that the average American worker had his own car.

They have heard a lot about racial discrimination. When non-Communist Russians eagerly asked about America, almost always they asked, "How about the Negroes?" They read daily of lynchings and murders of colored people in the United States, and they believed, as a consequence, that the Negroes' lot was as bad as that of the prisoners in Russia. There is a deep reason behind the question. They know that the only help in destroying communism they ever can expect is American help. When communism is overthrown, the United States will have some say in Russian affairs, and these men fear that they will be treated as they believe the Negroes are treated in America.

The people of the Soviet know that the government plays loose with the truth. Coal production in Mine 16 was 600 tons a day. Yet our published norm, which we always fulfilled on paper, was 1000 tons. Lying about production figures (in every phase of Soviet economy) goes all the way up the Soviet scale, and nobody takes them seriously. One day one of the free workers came

134

running in with a copy of the *Kutchigarka* (the *Stoker*), the local Vorkuta newspaper. "Comrades, look how good we are," he said, laughing. "They say Mine 16 has hit a record production of 2500 tons!"

Actually it never went higher than 900. One of the department managers sat down in the washroom with me one evening and thumbed through a copy of *Pravda*. He pointed out article after article, "That's not true. That's a lie. That's not true either."

19 THE WASHROOM

was not only an intellectual delight and a place to keep warm. It was a bathing place for the wives of the Red officials; none of them had showers or baths in their homes. They came in once a week. Most of them were young, and a few of them quite goodlooking. I gave them soap and a towel while they undressed right in the foyer of the washroom in front of me. Soviet women are not modest. They took off their dresses, slips, and ankle socks worn over rayon stockings (black cotton in the winter), and stood around talking to me in their brassieres and panties. Then, in the privacy of their bath they undressed completely. Russian women are exceedingly buxom. As they get older and heavier their heft is no particular adornment, but some of the young girls are attractive.

The days the women came in to bathe, the washroom was crowded with free workers and executives who had flocked in on the pretext of having to speak with me. They stood around, watching the women disrobe and passing vulgar wisecracks. "Oh, that one is real nice," an engineer said about one of the partially nude bathers. The young lady wisecracked back just as glibly.

The slave laborers working on the mine surface stared at the women entering the bathhouse as if they were visitors from another planet. Two men climbed into the attic of the washroom and drilled holes in the ceiling directly over the bath the women used. They spent two months in the *bor* for their week of short-lived pleasure.

Life in the washroom was better than any I had known in Vorkuta. In fact, conditions improved for everyone a little. In 1952, the MVD decided on a bold plan. They started to pay the slaves a small salary. Starvation, low morale, and self-disablement had hurt coal production badly and the Kremlin hoped a few rubles' incentive might help.

My pay in the washroom was approximately 410 rubles a month, out of which the camp took almost 300 rubles for my "room and board," and another fee for the camp administration. I was paying for my own imprisonment! Of the remaining 110 rubles, I paid 22 a month in "withholding" income taxes to the Soviet government. The rest, about 88 rubles, was mine to spend. This was $22 at the official rate but, in purchasing power, much closer to $6.

Workers down in the mine who oversubscribed their "norms" sometimes earned 130 or 150 rubles, but they were allowed to draw only 100 of it, less taxes. Those who didn't fulfill their "norms" were paid nothing and were put on killing punishment rations besides.

The extra few rubles gave our slave camp some superficial aspects of civilization. In the camp canteen we bought tea, margarine, sugar, and marmalade for snacks after the slightly reduced evening meal. On free days we could go to the "restaurant" to buy extra cabbage soup, *kasha,* or fish. But the extra money didn't go very far.

Many men used much of their salary for prostitution, others for pure alcohol (at 130 rubles a pint!) which, when fixed with tea, was a powerful antidote for Vorkuta monotony. I drank this polar moonshine only once. Seeing embittered slave laborers a little tipsy and cutting up like teen-agers was strange enough. On my twenty-eighth birthday the Hungarian doctor bought a pint of alcohol for the occasion. I contributed a can of sliced Mexican pineapple which had cost me the equivalent of $4.00, and we had a festive time.

Even the *gornyaki,* the most dull-witted coal miners, who used to crouch in their two-and-one-half-foot-high tunnels, seemed to come out of their living death a little.

The Soviet incentive plan worked, in that Vorkuta coal production rose 20 percent. But it backfired dramatically in another, more vital way. As half-starved animals we had no strength or courage to protest. With fuller bellies we looked objectively at our plight for the first time. We were fed up with the inhuman working and living conditions, the impossible cold, the persecution by the blatnois, the MVD *stukachey,* the long winter nights, the monotony, and mostly the hopelessness.

20 MANY OF THE

free people and the guard component were as fed up with Arctic isolation as were the prisoners. There was bitter conflict between the "red boards," the Red army men, who were responsible for guarding the area outside the barbed wire, and the "blue boards," the MVD who handled camp policing and administration.

"The MVD get six times our pay, and many of them live in town with their wives," a Red army soldier once told me. "They have dancing, movies, vodka and women. We live here in barracks not much better than yours. This winter, ten boys standing guard on the tundra have committed suicide already."

The Red army looked on the MVD as glorified policemen and jailers, and the hostility often broke out into fist fights. Basically, the army enlisted men were sympathetic with the slaves.

Our own discontent was unorganized. We had groups formed strictly along national lines, but they were not united. The Baltic peoples had the strongest organizations (only a compatriot could share their bacon) and the Russians the weakest. The MVD found it difficult to plant informers among the Balts, but they had a few Russian *stukachey* still loyal to the Kremlin ("The regime has made a mistake in *my* case," they said) who heavily infiltrated the Russian groups.

There was no central slave-laborer organization to coordinate such a mad dream as a rebellion. Each camp was separated from the other by a twelve-foot fence and a hundred yards of tundra. Our only contact was through transferred prisoners, whom we always interrogated thoroughly for news outside our mine group. There was obviously no communications system for a full-scale uprising against General Derevyenko and the Kremlin.

There were isolated bits of sabotage. In Mine 7 a few spirited ex-Communist Soviet students stole dynamite sticks from the coal-blasting department, a few at a time. When they had stolen enough they blew up their power station and blasted one of the mine shafts. Then, from a prisoner transferred from Camp 2, I heard how 2000 men had organized to clean out the blatnois.

"We were almost rid of the tattooed monkeys," this slave told me. "Little by little the murderers in our camp were released or sent to Novaya Zemlya, and we had some peace. Then, one day, over a hundred more were brought in, and split up about five to a barracks. The MVD lieutenant said there was no separate barracks for them. The first day, one of the blatnois in my barracks put his open *shapka* (cap) down on a stool and said: 'I want it full of rubles when I return in an hour.' Many were afraid, and it was full when he came back. Then the next day the same, and again the next. Soon it was getting too much even for the cowards among us.

"We developed a plan. Those in the mine stole copper wire there and the electricians made bells from homemade parts. We connected the barracks with an alarm system. Then, one night, about three A.M., it rang throughout Camp 2. At the same instant, every barracks overpowered its handful of blatnois and took away their knives and hatchets. We emptied one of our barracks and locked all the blatnois in. We poured stolen gasoline over it and lit a fire. If it were not for the guards who put out the flame and freed the blatnois they would all have burned for their crimes. But we were rid of them anyway. They were all shipped out the next day."

But rebelling against the blatnois and rebelling against the Soviet government were obviously jobs of different dimensions. The Vorkuta intelligentsia sat around dreaming of a rebellion or a mass strike against the Kremlin

139

but the average Russian just couldn't understand such a concept.

"They are mad dreamers," one *moujik* (peasant) who had fought Soviet collectivization in the 'thirties told me. "I have lived under the Communists for thirty-five years and I have never seen anyone oppose them and win. What have we to rebel with? Our bare hands?"

The moujik made sense. Yet, within a few months' time three closely related incidents were to set the stage for a dramatic, violent uprising of 100,000 slaves of Vorkuta —the first rebellion against the Soviet monolith in thirty-five years and one of the most significant political events of modern times.

Stalin, not Derevyenko, Beria, or even the cold, was our mortal enemy. Each of us felt personally imprisoned by the "Moustache," or the "Old One," as he was often called. We painstakingly studied his most recent pictures in *Pravda*. One slave hopefully commented: "He doesn't look too well to me. See his eyes—how old and tired they are."

Then, the first days of March, came the news we had waited so long to hear. Stalin had been stricken with an apoplectic fit. "May the devil take his soul today!" the prisoners prayed, on their knees. The morning of March 6, 1953, his death was announced over the loudspeaker in Mine 16.

I stood among a mixed crowd of soot-covered slave laborers, free workers, and Red officials and watched their expressions. My fellow slaves lit up with hope. "He lived too long—the old dog," one prisoner yelled. An old man got down on his knees in the water. "Thank God, someone still looks out for the wretched." The faces of the free

140

people were immobile. No one uttered a word of praise for the dead dictator.

The next day, the cautious administration had Stalin's portrait removed from the front of the coal locomotive and replaced it with Lenin's picture. "Who knows?" one of the department managers commented to me in the washroom. "In a few months' time maybe the old one will be called a traitor."

Stalin's death sent a wave of frenzied expectation throughout Vorkuta. "Maybe Uncle Zhorka [Malenkov, the new premier] will close all the slave camps and free us all?" Vaska asked me one day. "What do you think, Johnny?"

I wasn't quite that optimistic, but for the first time in its history, Vorkuta awaited each new day hopefully. The first months of Malenkov's regime, however, were surprisingly uneventful. The release of the Jewish doctors whom Stalin had falsely accused of plotting murder was one good sign.

On April 14, Beria's birthday, we heard rumors of a general amnesty. "Don't believe it, Johnny," one of the old-timers in my barracks said. "It's only more *parasha*" (latrine rumors). Later that day, an amnesty was declared by Beria for all prisoners serving five-year sentences or less. But it was only a shallow bid for national popularity that hardly affected a single political prisoner. In all, 5000 men were released from Vorkuta, mostly blatnois and workers arrested for chronic absenteeism. Eight hundred of the released blatnois were soon back in camp after they had started a murderous wave of robberies and knife stabbings in town, killing 1200.

The free workers spoke almost lovingly about the new

premier. In a short time, the amount of consumer goods —shoes, shirts, suits, bicycles, clocks—in the stores of Vorkuta and the *posiyoloks* had almost doubled. Prices too had dropped.

But in Camp 3, Mine 16, slave life went on unchanged. We waited for some word, some sign from Malenkov or Beria rejecting the slave brutality of Stalin. But it never came.

April and May, bitter, disappointing months, passed without change. Vorkuta rumbled badly and the sabotage became more frequent. We were ready for trouble of some kind. We needed only a spark to set it off.

This came in June—two events, hard on the heels of each other. Early in the month, over Radio Moscow, we heard of the arrest of our jailer, MVD chief L. P. Beria, for "treason." (He was executed on September 23, 1953.) The news of Beria's arrest shocked the local MVD administration. Every "Blue" from Derevyenko down to lowly *nadsiratel* (guard) expected to follow Beria into Lubianka or perhaps become one of us for participation in Beria's plot—whatever that may have been. A few of the guards nervously asked us: "What do you think will happen now?"

It wasn't clearly defined until later, but the MVD detachment in Camp 3, as well as throughout all the U.S.S.R., became openly split. In private conversation, some admitted loyalty to Beria, others to Premier Malenkov. Beria's arrest became a powerful catalyst, and the ground swell of tension rose to the surface. Slaves began insulting the administration and the MVD informers more openly. "We're cowards," one Estonian in my barracks said one day. "The Kremlin can't control itself, but a half million of us in Vorkuta jump when they sneeze."

142

On June 18 we heard even more startling news. My friend Ivan came rushing over to my shelf. "Johnny, it's in *Pravda*. The East Germans have rebelled. Come look for yourself." I joined a group crowded around a copy of *Pravda* pasted on the wall. Someone was reading the story out loud. *Pravda* naturally blamed the East German riots on American subversion, but the story of strike against higher norms and the open fighting in the streets of Berlin was surprisingly candid. Every time the article mentioned the Berliners' resistance, we cheered. Their spirit inspired us and we discussed nothing else for days after. (Months later, some 200 heroes of that day, East Berlin boys from sixteen to twenty-two, arrived in Vorkuta to start five- to twenty-year terms as slave laborers.)

The next month we were cocky slaves. The long summer sun had melted the snow, and its warmth was renewing our energy and courage. We discussed the chance of striking for our freedom, but no one seemed to know what to do. Many men, especially the Russians who were deathly afraid of informers, were unable to make a decision.

Fortunately it was made for us. The morning of July 21, when I reported to the washroom, one of the department managers spoke to me.

"It's finally come, Amerikanitz. Mines 17 and 18 are on strike. Derevyenko himself went into the barracks and asked them to go back to work. They just laughed.

"But don't think it will do Camp 3 any good," he goaded me. "Everyone has to fight for his own freedom."

At 5:00 A.M. that morning, the workers of Mine 17 had fallen out for *rasvod*, the morning roll call, with secret instructions from an elected leader not to report to work. They demanded to be taken back to the barracks instead of to the mine. "When the barbed wire comes down," one of them told the guard, "we'll mine coal again. Not until." The guards tried to be firm, but without specific instructions from Derevyenko to shoot, they knew there was nothing they could do.

21 REPORTS OF THE strike in Mine 17 soon traveled throughout our Mine 16. All during the day, rumors kept coming in through the free workers. The strike had spread to Mines 9, 10, and 25. There was more talk than work that day. "Amerikanitz, do you think it's true or is it just more *parasha?*" one of the men asked me that night. I knew it was true. "Shuisky told me in the washroom," I said. "He's a good Communist and they want to prove that they're well informed."

The next day, July 22, the skeptics were convinced. Mine 7 in the camp next to us had joined the strike. The wheels in their mine elevator were not turning. For a while full coal cars came through (the rail line went through our mine). But later that day, the Mine 7 coal cars were three-fourths empty, and emblazoned in chalk across the inside of each car in big bold Russian letters was written: "TO HELL WITH YOUR COAL. WE WANT FREEDOM." There were hand-written leaflets pasted all over the cars, addressed to us. "Comrades from Mines 12, 14, and 16. Don't let us down. You know we are striking."

Immediately we formed our own strike committee. Our strike leader was Gureyvich, the Russian Jew and former

144

Soviet diplomat. His committee was made up mostly of Russian intellectuals, some still Marxist, but all violently anti-Soviet. One of them, a Russian German, once had a trading post in the Volga. Although he had been pro-Stalin in attitude, he was summarily imprisoned during World War II along with thousands of Russians of German ancestry.

That night a few members of the committee came to see me in my barracks. "We haven't decided when to go out with the others, Amerikanitz," Gureyvich confided, "but when we do, you will have one of the most important jobs. It will be your responsibility to convince the Red department managers not to interfere. They respect you as an American—no one has forgotten all the equipment and food your country sent over during the war."

I had a chance to put the plan into effect the very next morning. The second week in July, fifty prison boxcars filled with slaves, guarded by a tender car bristling with machine guns, had arrived in Vorkuta. The prisoners were from the Karaganda slave camp in Kazakhstan Republic in southeastern U.S.S.R. They were being sent north because of the acute labor shortage in Vorkuta. Some 20 percent of all our slaves were now cripples. As an inducement the Karagandas had been promised higher wages and resettlement in Vorkuta as free exiles, with excellent housing.

But the government had lied. The Karagandas were split up among the Vorkuta camps and settled as regular prisoners. About two hundred were brought into our Camp 3. That morning, July 24, the Karagandas in our camp, aware of strikes going on elsewhere, refused to work unless the government promises were carried out. One of the promises was that they would be issued

145

mining clothes, which slaves did not have. When the Karagandas refused to work in their regular clothes, the brigadiers went to the storeroom with them, to see what they could find. No order was passed on for the Karagandas to receive the clothing, and so they stood about, protesting.

Meanwhile, the workers down in the mine were awaiting instructions concerning their work. The free engineers and supervisors, who wanted to line things up so that production could start rolling, had to change into overalls before going down into the mines. To change, they had to come to my department, which meant that my role in helping to start the strike was about to begin.

The first department manager to come in was, luckily, one of the friendliest. He looked around, spotted me, and patted me on the back, saying, "At last you fellows have courage enough to put up some resistance. I'd better go home; I need sleep."

"Wait," I begged him. "Try to take your twin along with you." The "twin" was an exceedingly hard-boiled Communist. Both men were abnormally short, hence the nickname. I had hardly spoken when the other "twin" hurried in, ready to rush into the mine and get things organized.

"Are you crazy?" his companion said. "The slaves will kill you. You'll be lucky if they shut you up for a day or so in the elevator. Why don't you come along with me? I've got a bottle at home, and when we reach the bottom we won't know who's who, anyhow!"

They both laughed and went out together. More engineers came in, one after another, some cursing, some grinning. I reached for their overcoats and had these on

146

their backs before they knew what was happening. I opened the door, bade them a very pleasant weekend, and ushered them out. Without a word, but with a nod or a wink, they left for home. None left with his overalls, none went to the mine.

Only the boss, the executive engineer, was still unaccounted for, but not for long. "Where are all my engineers?" I heard him shout. He had poked his head in the dressing-room door.

"Why, they've all left," I said. "The mine is at a standstill, and they have nothing to do."

"Now what?" was all he had to say. Holding his overcoat for him, I suggested that he call off the second shift and send the first shift home. They were only costing him money, I said, and there was no production anyway. He left with a curse, called off the second shift, and never came back till the storm was over.

I fell back on the dressing bench in relief. "Thank God they're gone," I said to myself. My job was done. It wasn't much of a job, really, but it helped.

I left with the rest of the first shift. Back in the camp, everyone wanted to know how it had started.

Meanwhile, posters with strikers' demands were being put up throughout the camp. The strike date was set for July 25. But it was only the twenty-fourth, and the strike was already underway.

Our strike slogan was "Not an ounce of coal for the plan." A list of demands was drawn up: 1. Removal of the barbed wire. 2. Barracks to be kept unlocked at night. 3. Release for all charged with violations in connection with the war. 4. Release of all political prisoners who had served ten years or more in Russian prisons. (I had served

147

nine!) 5. Thorough check of the trial of all political prisoners. Release of the innocent. For the rest, setting of new lower sentences in accordance with international law.

"I think we have valuable allies," one member of the strike committee confided to me. I soon saw what he meant. I spotted one of the MVD guards coming out of our outhouse. I walked in after he left, and pasted high on the wall was a printed strike leaflet that hadn't been there a minute before. We have excellent allies, indeed, I thought. Some of Beria's loyal underlings had obviously helped to start our revolt or were using it to their own advantage to foment discontent against the Malenkov regime.

Meanwhile thirty of the Karagandas who had refused to work that morning were arrested by Tchevchenko. Immediately Gureyvich, the strike committee, and some 2000 other prisoners stormed down toward the prison. We stood before the gate, called out strike slogans, and yelled: "Free the Karagandas!" Major Tchevchenko, with his perennially sickly appearance, came out and tried to calm us.

"There is no cause for trouble, men. I promise that the Karagandas will be released before six o'clock tonight."

It was then 3:15 P.M. We decided to wait and see. But a few minutes later, several *chornie vorons* (police wagons; literally, "black ravens,") drove up with several police cars and four truckloads of troops. They had obviously come to take the Karagandas off Tchevchenko's hands and bring them to the central prison. About one hundred Red army and MVD troops commanded by our harsh MVD lieutenant of restriction, who had been in Vorkuta only two weeks, piled out of the trucks and surrounded the camp gates.

We cursed violently and almost in unison, and shoulder to shoulder rushed to bar the troops' way into the camp. We were successful. They had to retreat. A "stool pigeon" showed up among us and tried to persuade us to let the troops in to take the men. He had hardly begun talking when a mob rushed him. He was taken off to the hospital. The MVD men tried a new plan to lay hold of the thirty Karagandas. Since the *bor* was off limits, it was possible for the MVD to cut through the fence and reach the *bor* from the rear. As soon as we saw what was going on, a new wave of protest shattered the air.

Suddenly, the thirty Karaganda prisoners, who had overcome their three drunken guards, dashed out of the prison into the yard. We set up a tremendous yell of jubilation. A second later, the MVD lieutenant ordered: "Open fire!"

I was pinned against the administration building fifty yards from the troops, caught in a crossfire of sub-machine-gun and rifle bullets. I pressed flat against the wall and mumbled a prayer. From where I stood I could see that all fifty Red army men and a few of the MVD had disobeyed the lieutenant and were not firing. Next to the lieutenant a Red army soldier had his submachine barrel pointed stubbornly down to the ground. The MVD lieutenant put away his own pistol, impatiently grabbed the soldier's weapon and started firing.

The firing lasted only twenty seconds, but it seemed like eternity. When it was over, fifteen of our men lay wounded on the ground. Two were dead, and others were taken away to die. One of the two dead men, due to be released in only two months, had the top of his head blown off just in front of me by an explosive bullet fired by Molkov, the hated guard. A stray bullet went through the hospital window and punctured the lung of a patient in bed. I turned to look at the wall behind me. Two feet over my head, a submachine gun had cut a twisted pattern of bullet holes in the wall of the building.

We were enraged. After looking at the dead and wounded, Gureyvich signaled to some of the committee, and together they walked to the front gate. Staring into the muzzles of a hundred guns, Gureyvich addressed Tchevchenko, Buikoff, the lieutenant, and all the guards in a sharp commanding voice.

"The strike committee is officially relieving you of command of Camp 3 and Mines 12, 14, and 16," he said. "From this moment on, we prisoners will be in complete charge. No officers or guards will be allowed within the gate without permission of the strike committee. If the lieutenant or Molkov attempts to enter, he will be killed without a hearing. If you want to stop us, you will have to shoot all forty-five hundred prisoners now. Meanwhile not an ounce of coal comes out of the pits for Leningrad." We cheered our hearts out.

It worked. No one fired, no one raised a defiant hand to stop us. Only the young woman *feldshar* was allowed in to care for the wounded. Within a few minutes, we had rounded up three MVD guards and a senior lieutenant still lurking in the camp area, and unceremoniously kicked them out the front gate. With a touch of courage, our coal strike had been transformed into an uprising. The great Vorkuta Slave Rebellion of 1953 had begun.

We immediately formed what was, for all practical purposes, an independent slave republic. A member of the strike committee was put in charge of each barracks. A young Russian graduate of a Soviet technical school was put in command of mine. All the food in the *stolovaya*, the canteen, and the restaurant was commandeered, and new higher rations were set for all. The prisoners in the *bor* were released. We appointed our own police, but it was hardly necessary. Perfect discipline was maintained. The separate national groups became welded into one. The morale of the men, exhilarated by the fresh breath of freedom, was fantastically high. We would gladly have all died together to keep it.

Not one of our 4500 men worked the mines, including the brigadiers and *desetnicks*. A few free workers were permitted to man the pits—to work the ventilators and keep the hallways clear of coal gas, and to pump excess water out—but not one lump of coal was allowed to be removed.

During the entire melee, the once-fierce blatnois sulked in their barracks like spanked youngsters. They were completely unable to decipher what strange force had turned their world upside down and robbed them of their power.

Seven known informers were dragged from their barracks and brought down to the front gate. We threw them to the MVD outside. "Here are your *stukachey*," Gureyvich told Captain Buikoff. "We can't guarantee their lives in here."

Not long after the shooting, we made our own flag, a plain Red banner (the hammer and sickle is the Communist Party flag) bordered in black cloth in memory of our two murdered comrades. We raised it at half-mast on a tall pole over the *stolovaya*. Fifteen minutes later, from the electric power station across the hill, another red-and-black flag, an exact duplicate of ours, rose—magically, it seemed—up a pole into the sun. A few minutes later, it happened at Mine 7. Then, one at a time, as far as the eye could see across the tundra, the new red-and-black

151

banner of slaves-made-free replaced the Soviet flag over much of Vorkuta.

We kept in contact with the other camps through the sympathetic free workers. In this way the strike demands of each camp were almost exactly the same. We unanimously agreed to deal only with a representative of the Politburo in Moscow or with a member of the Central Communist Party Committee.

We learned that the pattern of strike followed by an insurrection had taken place in most of the camps. They too had driven the MVD out the gate and assumed complete control of everything within the barbed wires. In Mine 40, the largest and most modern in Vorkuta, there had also been MVD violence. A few men were shot defying the order to go to work. From our sources, we knew that the electric power station, the railroad camp, and some thirty-five coal camps had joined the uprising. Between 85,000 and 100,000 slaves were on strike.

The Kremlin was paralyzed in its own internal power struggle and afraid to issue definite orders on how to handle the slave rebellion—other than with "extreme caution." We knew that Malenkov's nervous, unstable new regime needed the coal badly and could not afford to have the uprising spread.

The MVD ranks in Vorkuta were split. Some officers and men (who they were—perhaps Tchevchenko himself —were known only to the strike leaders) were helping us by adding to the official paralysis. Their hope was that the rebellion would spread throughout the slave empire and act as a lever to unseat Malenkov, free Beria, or at least protect his appointees from extinction.

We heard that similar uprisings were taking place

through the 20,000,000-slave GULAG slave region. Eighty-one Japanese slave laborers from Karaganda who have recently returned home corroborated this. Two hundred slaves in their camp had been cut down by tanks and machine guns in a small but similar uprising that summer. Free people later brought us news that our uprising sparked strikes everywhere: in the Ural ore mines, in the coal mines outside Moscow, on the enormous collective farms of the Ukraine.

Later in the afternoon of the first day of the strike, three hundred soldiers were deployed around our camp in newly dug trenches. I could see machine guns and mortars being put in place.

At 6:30 P.M. Captain Buikoff requested permission to enter the camp. He came through the gates unarmed and unescorted and read a statement from General Derevyenko.

"As of yesterday, July 23, 1953," Buikoff began (the veins in his thick neck stood out in embarrassment), "all prisoners will receive up to three hundred rubles a month compensation. The bars are to be removed from the windows of the barracks, the barracks will no longer be locked in the evening, evening roll call will be eliminated. With the permission of the commanding officer, prisoners may receive visitors from home once a year."

The men listened, smiles spread across their faces, as Buikoff continued his list of official concessions. The slave numbers were no longer required on our clothing; an attempt would be made to provide better housing, food, and clothing. Soviet citizens could mail letters once a month instead of twice a year. (I still couldn't write a postcard.)

From what he said, the same concessions were being

153

made to all the striking camps. Buikoff finished the statement without one word about our returning to work, then turned on his heel and walked out.

Up to triple pay! No more bars! We cheered lustily. The rebellion was only a few hours old, and the nervous administration had already granted us important concessions. We rushed to the barracks, shouting and yelling, and ripped the bars from the windows with our bare hands.

"Come, Amerikanitz, give me a hand," one of the Ukrainians called. He was pulling the hinges off the door that held the heavy iron crossbar lock in place. Some were joyfully tearing the slave numbers off their clothes. Others, however, said, "No, I will keep my number on until this number doesn't exist any more." On paper the number existed as before, even if it was ripped off the clothing. My number, 1-E-241, was reserved for me whether I wore it or not. Later, punishment was threatened for all who did not want to take it off. But many men felt lost without a number on their clothes. Their stupid, dead life had become a formula and they had forgotten how to think. They took the wrong clothing by mistake —and it really didn't matter: clothes were all alike, anyhow, and no one had the right size to begin with.

The next three days, July 25, 26, and 27, were pure bliss. Nature had joined forces with us and granted us cloudless sunny days. The temperature hit 70 degrees. All over Camp 3, men basked on the tundra soaking up the sun and discussing the amazing chain of events. I sat with friends by the fence, and we congratulated ourselves on our luck thus far. A Red army soldier patrolling in front of us stopped and asked through the gate: "What's going on? Have you gained anything?" We told him about

Derevyenko's concessions and our good life these last three days. "Good," he answered. "We're on your side. I don't care if you strike until doomsday. No Red army men will ever fire on you."

Actually we were biding time, waiting for a Kremlin representative, the only one who could agree to a reduction of sentences. But Moscow had kept perfect silence.

On July 27, Derevyenko himself, a short, stocky man of fifty with a gray-haired crew cut, came to speak with us, accompanied by Dochtin, the Minister of Internal Affairs for the Komi Republic. They too were unarmed and unescorted, although, of course, there were 300 troops with mortars and machine guns directly outside the fence.

They continued the kid-glove treatment that had thus far characterized the official attitude. Derevyenko walked from one group to another, talking in a fatherly, solicitous manner. "Don't you think it would be best to go back to work in the mines?" he asked me and the others. "You have won most of your demands. What more do you want?"

"We are waiting for the Kremlin," a member of the strike committee told him. Just before he left the camp, Derevyenko announced that MVD General Masslennikov, holder of the Order of Lenin and Deputy Minister of Internal Affairs for the entire Soviet Union, was flying up from Moscow to talk with us.

Masslennikov's visit, one of the free workers told us, was the result of six days' frantic pleading by Derevyenko for Moscow to take a firm stand.

The news was heralded as another strike victory, but I believe many of us, deep in our hearts, were worried. Masslennikov had a reputation for both shrewdness and cruelty.

The next day, the twenty-eighth, another beautiful day,

155

we buried our two dead. Fifty free women from the *posi-yolok* a half mile away were waiting at the gate to throw flowers on the funeral truck. I thought it was a fine symbol of sympathy with our stand. The burial was on the open football field, where four and a half thousand of us, wearing black mourning ribbons cut from what once was our slave numbers, filed by to pay our respects.

22 ON THE TWENTY-
ninth, at noon, Ivan ran into my barracks. "Get up, Johnny! The Moscow general, Masslennikov! He's coming down the road!" I got off my shelf and ran down to the gate just in time to see a long black car drive into camp between two lines of one hundred heavily armed guards. Masslennikov got out, and the limousine made a U-turn and parked between the lines of MVD troops, its nose pointed toward the open gate. Outside there were at least five hundred troops patrolling.

An entourage of thirty officers, mostly colonels, followed Masslennikov to the football field, where we had set chairs and a long table for them in advance.

They had come ostensibly to hear our demands, and we were quite ready for them. The strike committee had chosen twenty speakers to present our viewpoint. Four and a half thousand slaves in one strong mass were assembled on the football field facing the Kremlin brass. I had a choice position up front.

It was the most stirring scene I had ever witnessed in

156

my life. First, Gureyvich presented our demands for review and reduction of sentences, and freedom for all men who had served ten years. Then, from the ranks, one man at a time stepped out to speak—lowly slave laborers given a chance to pour out to one of the Soviet's mightiest their bile about Red indecency. And presumably Masslennikov had to listen.

The speeches were moving, intelligent, and biting. A former professor of history of the University of Leningrad said, in starting, that he knew it would mean an extra ten years as a slave. Masslennikov protested violently: "Nyet, nyet. You can all speak freely." The professor did. He traced the history of slavery from pre-Pharaoh times, through the slave trade on the Gold Coast. "But never in the story of man," he said, "has working slavery been so extensive or so cruelly exploited as here in the Soviet Union—the 'liberator' of the working class!"

We passionately cheered each word. "Vot! Vot! That's it! That's it!" I yelled with the others.

The next speaker was a former Red army officer. "I was raised under communism and wanted no other way," he began. "During the war I was decorated many times. I took seventeen bullet wounds and returned to fight again. The eighteenth time I was wounded I fell unconscious on the field. When I came to, I was a German prisoner. I escaped and spent the rest of the war fighting the Nazis with a band of Soviet partisans. In 1946, when our government learned I had once been a German prisoner of war, I was sentenced to twenty years in Vorkuta. Now I have come to the conclusion that communism breeds only slavery."

A Pole spoke for the foreigners. Two former high Soviet bureaucrats spoke about the abuse of Marxist doctrine and its perversion in the Soviet Union. It was an exhilarating experience, listening to free men speak their minds, if only for a few minutes.

Masslennikov was pale. He listened with head bent forward for over an hour. He was obviously shocked. In his thirty years of bolshevism, he had never heard such words uttered publicly. He never spoke, except to interrupt occasionally. "Remember, you are insulting the great Soviet Union." When the speeches were over, he got up and left for the next camp without a word.

Masslennikov completed his rounds of the striking camps the next day without making a dent in the strikers' unity. None of the camps had agreed to return to work. The uneasy truce continued. The slaves rested, but they were not relaxed. They joked, but the jokes covered up internal restlessness.

Then, on August 1, three days after our meeting on the football field and exactly ten days since the beginning of the strike, I was coming out of the *stolovaya* at 6 A.M., after breakfast, when I saw something strange. The men of Mine 7 were being removed from the camp and taken out into the tundra in small groups under heavy guard. After about thirty groups had been assembled, they started to return, one group at a time, to the camp.

An hour later we found out what had happened. The MVD had let the first group of Mine 7 men go back to camp without a word. "You see," they told the second group, "the first group has agreed to return to work. Will you follow their example and report at the pits this morning, or do we have to shoot you all now, right here on the tundra?" One MVD officer asked each group the same question by prearranged order.

That broke the strike in Mine 7. The MVD troops who

had executed the threat were not from Vorkuta. They were part of a special guards regiment of 1200 MVD men brought in by Masslennikov to quell the rebellion.

At 9 A.M. General Masslennikov drove up to our gate and asked for Gureyvich. His battalion was deployed on the tundra in battle formation.

"You can see the elevator wheels are already turning in Mine 7. It would be wisest to follow their example," Masslennikov said. "The ultimatum is work or death."

Gureyvich pondered a few seconds. "Give us twenty-four hours to think it over," he said.

Masslennikov looked at him distrustfully, but answered, "Agreed." As events turned out, Gureyvich's mastery of the diplomatic stall had saved the lives of many of us.

From our camp, Masslennikov and his troops moved up the road to Mine 29 on the hill next to us. We were cut off from events for over an hour. Then, at eleven o'clock we heard a violent outburst of gunfire that filled the empty tundra for two full minutes. A few minutes later there was a call for all camp doctors to rush to Mine 29. Masslennikov had broken the back of their rebellion with a blood bath.

Later, I was able to reconstruct the scene. Masslennikov had driven up to the camp gates in a car equipped with a loudspeaker, backed by his 1200 troops surrounding the fences. Two and a half thousand slaves, arms locked, were packed in front of the gates.

"Go back to your barracks!" Masslennikov called over the loudspeaker. "Follow the example of the other mines. They are already working in the pits." The crowd yelled back insults and crowded closer to the fence.

At Masslennikov's hand signal, a squad of troops pushed open the gates and advanced single file about fifteen feet

159

into the camp. But as the prisoners walked toward them defiantly, they turned and ran. A few minutes later, two giant fire hoses were pushed through the side fences. Four bulky Ukrainian prisoners rushed over and jammed the nozzles shut. When the pumps were turned on, the water trickled harmlessly on the tundra.

"I warn you, go back to your barracks!" Masslennikov ordered again. When no one moved, the MVD chief decided to try psychological persuasion.

"All those who want to return to work, come outside the gate."

Every prisoner's eye swung in a circle around him and glared as fifty men of the 2500 walked out.

Masslennikov looked disgustedly at the small group and yelled: "Get back in!"

He called out on the loudspeaker the third time. "End this rebellion now. Go back to your barracks. Organize yourselves to work. This is the last warning I will give you." Even before Masslennikov had completed his tirade, the slaves chanted back, "To hell with your coal. If you won't give us freedom, we'll take it ourselves!"

As the prisoners stood by the gate, the heavy machine guns, set up twenty yards from the fence, and the massed infantry opened fire. The machine-gun staccato punctuated the screams of the wounded for two full minutes until no one was left standing. Blood was over everyone. One hundred and ten had been killed instantly. More than five hundred were seriously wounded. Masslennikov ordered the gates opened and barked orders to the living to come out on the tundra. Those who still refused to work would be killed on the spot. The survivors wailed as they stepped over the bodies of their fallen comrades and walked toward the gate.

160

The next day, when we learned of the Red bloodletting, we too returned to work. Then, one at a time, an hour or so apart, other camps surrendered to the MVD. By late that afternoon, the uprising was over.

The next week, the MVD made up in severity for its indecision during the strike. Every few hours another man was dragged away and sent to a central *bor* set up for strike leaders. In all, 7000 Vorkuta slaves were arrested, 300 from my camp. Three MVD officers and two guards from Camp 3 were also arrested and charged with helping to inspire the rebellion. Colonel Burtiev, one of Derevyenko's chief assistants, was discharged from the MVD.

Of the 7000 seized, 300 were executed without a trial. One thousand men were transferred to the Far East, and the rest were given additional three-to-five-year sentences. These, with the exception of a few, were never seen or heard of again. I never again saw Gureyvich or the heroes who had so eloquently spoken for us that day.

I worried myself half sick all during the bloody week of retaliation, waiting to be taken in with the others. All it would take was one word from anyone on the strike committee who knew my role. But they went to their Maker without incriminating me.

23

BY OUR WESTERN standards, I presume, the slave rebellion was a failure. We had struck for freedom and we were still GULAG slaves. But that is an oversimplification. The mere fact that the rebellion took place at all in the Soviet Union made it an instantaneous, glorious success. Its effect on the Communist world was electrifying. The people of Leningrad, in letters to free workers in Vorkuta, expressed sympathy with our cause. Just as the East Berlin riots drove the Soviet to a more conciliatory attitude toward its satellites, so we 100,000 slaves in those ten days showed the Kremlin that its own internal solidarity is a sham, a carefully poised egg that must be handled gingerly. If nothing else, the story of this first organized resistance to the Soviet mammoth in thirty-five years, this strike of slave workers in the "worker's paradise," has traveled the interminable Russian grapevine and given hope to 20,000,-000 GULAG slaves and perhaps not a few of communism's "free workers."

Vorkuta never quieted down. A triumphant spirit, buoyed up by the wage increase we had won, was the strike's heritage. In February 1954, a section of the office building in Mine 7 was blown up by a homemade bomb. Then the generator of the electric power station was partially destroyed. An MVD search of our mine turned up 400 sticks of dynamite planted to blow up the main elevator shaft.

In 1954, in a shift of slaves planned to weaken our prisoner organizations, I was moved into Mine 29, the scene of the August 1 massacre. The men in my barracks proudly showed me the healed wounds of that day. Almost every man carried one or more scars, and bullet holes still gaped in every wall.

At this point I had lost all hope of an early release. I had been taken out of the washroom and put on a killing lumber job. During the strike, for no logical reason, I somehow expected a wildly careening chain of events that

162

would end up with me as a free man back in Detroit. But that dream was over, and there were eleven years left to my sentence. In all my time in Vorkuta, I had never been interrogated, and it disturbed me. There were times when I hoped for some official sign that they knew of my existence. God knows—I might become one of the "forgotten" men I had heard about, living out my life in slave camps, lost in the morass of Soviet bureaucracy.

I had just one glimmer of hope—a three-by-five piece of cardboard—a postcard they had never allowed me to send to my folks in the United States but which I had sent out over the name of another prisoner.

Only a selected few prisoners had the privilege of sending cards through the International Red Cross to their relatives. I was not one of these, and, besides, America was on its way to becoming world enemy No. 1, according to Soviet propagandists. One of the barbers in Camp 10, Rudi Rohrig, was one of the few (he also is free now). Rudi never received answers to the cards he sent; consequently, he didn't care about making full use of the privilege any more. Even so, he considered it dangerous to allow others to capitalize on his privilege. The censor knew so intimately the history of every prisoner that one could not hope to get away with writing to a new address.

Luckily, in May 1954 the censor was replaced by an old MVD colonel. Would he be as well informed as his predecessor? We decided to take the chance, although the card still would go out over the name of Rudi Rohrig. It was addressed to a distant relative of mine in West Germany.

A day or two after the card was mailed, Rudi had to go to shave the officers. The old colonel, under the straight razor, asked Rudi why he had written to others than his relatives—and why he had asked for everything under the sun. "They will think we really are poor when they get this card," he said.

"Well," Rudi said, "others make a little money in the mine, but I don't get anything extra to live on. And I had to write to neighbors, because my relatives never answer."

"If that's the case," said the colonel, "I'll let the card go out this time. But don't ever dare write a letter like that again."

We wondered if the card would get through; and, if it did, whether the recipients would rightly interpret the words "noble nephew" and send the card on to Detroit. They did send it to my family, but I did not learn this for more than half a year.

Early in June, I was eating my cabbage soup in the *stolovaya* when the *nevalney,* my barracks master, rushed in excitedly. "Amerikanitz, the camp commander is looking for you. You have orders to proceed to Moscow." I looked up at him and laughed in my soup. A few minutes later, a friend came in with the same news.

I rushed nervously to the Administration Building and stood at attention before MVD Lieutenant Antrashkevich. "You are to leave for Moscow at 7 A.M.," he said.

"To Moscow?" I asked.

"As far as I know, you're going home," Antrashkevich said.

I heard him, but the words didn't sink in. I wouldn't let them. The thought was wild. Why should I be released? There was no general amnesty. I had so lost touch with the world that Vorkuta and its regulations were the only reality I understood. But I prayed, just in case.

Very few prisoners of Arctic camps lived to see freedom. Few were transported back to Moscow. A few handfuls left in November or December 1953, but no one ever heard whether they were finally released or were held in some other camp. The American Homer Cox was among them.

Now that it was my turn to leave, I wondered what lay ahead.

A slip with fourteen questions had to be signed in the various departments—kitchen, bathroom, stockroom, library, office, and even the political branches.

I didn't get much sleep that night. Many men of the various nationalities came to me to ask if I would send word to their loved ones when I was free. Others wanted me to pass on to the free world the true condition of the slaves, so that their eyes might be opened and they might avoid a similar end.

There were others I should have liked to talk to a little more, so that I might give details to responsible authorities. Among these were some who had been only a few days in our camp, deported from their home town because they knew too much. They had lived close to the place where the first two Soviet atomic tests were made. The Kremlin gang did not want the world to know that the unfinished bombs and the laboratories were blasted. Foreign instruments recorded the explosion, and the Soviets were obliged to announce it as a successful test. Were all tests equally successful?

The sleepless hours of that night flew by, and before I knew it hundreds were up to wave farewell as I was marched to the railroad by an unarmed guard.

I was taken to Camp 15. Outside the gate a fellow slave worker was repairing the fence. "Te tagshay Amerikanitz?— Are you also an American?" he asked. I replied with a nod.

"We have two of your countrymen here who are also going away."

A few minutes later I met U.S. Army Privates Marchuk and Verdine. We rode together to the railway station. It was a pleasure to speak English again, although I was careful with every word I said. I did not know these two men, and their meeting me could be a trap. True, the Soviets knew I didn't share their view of life and would never become a Communist; also, I had committed no crime. There was nothing, therefore, to be afraid of, nothing to avoid talking about. But the years in Communist prisons had taught me that they will turn your words any way they want to, and for this reason I was on guard. I was particularly careful with Marchuk, because he spoke a very good Russian. Verdine, on the other hand, could not speak the language so fluently, and I felt more confidence in him.

Marchuk told me he had gotten drunk in a bar in Berlin and wandered across the Red border. Verdine said he had been kidnaped while on duty at the demarcation line.

As we spoke I kept thinking. "Why three Americans traveling together? Are we going to a special slave camp for Americans? Could there be another reason? Was there a chance that Antrashkevich was right?"

At the Vorkuta station, I walked right up to the parked Stalopinski and waited for the MVD officer walking behind me. He laughed: "No, no, Amerikanitz. That's not for you any more. Get in the train!"

The three of us, without handcuffs and accompanied by two MVD officers, traveled in a civilian passenger train from Vorkuta to Moscow.

The officers explained that they did not speak English, and so our conversation with them had to be in Russian. I

166

would have believed them if they had not fallen so easily into a trap. Sitting on the upper bench, which was for sleeping only, with Marchuk and Verdine, I asked the Americans what time it was. I kept my eyes on the Russian officers below. Automatically the officers looked at their watches. I knew, then, that they understood English.

It was to take four days to reach Moscow. Because there was no diner, we had cold meals. As we stopped at stations on the way, children and old women would run alongside the train, selling a hot potato, an egg, a ladle of milk. Chains of beggars filed through the cars, old and young, sick and blind, complaining that they had no work and no home. The officers kept them moving along, but it was obvious that, before us Americans, the beggars were a cause of embarrassment.

The officers did not seem to object, however, when girls and women traveling on the train undressed at night down to their underclothing before lying down to sleep. A very few had colorful pajamas, which they not only wore sleeping but when they left the train to shop along the platform. Even after we arrived in Moscow, some went into the street in their pajamas.

Moscow was a big change for us. A dozen or so MVD officials were at the station to receive us. We were escorted to a bus—which from the outside I recognized as a prison car with cells. This took us to Boutyrki, the Soviet Union's most elaborate prison. After all extras were taken from us, we were shown to our room. This was a large three-bed cell, with fresh sheets, all the comforts, and even a clean toilet pail.

The next day two colonels visited us. They asked how we were, and I, speaking for the three of us, asked what was coming next.

"You are not going back to a slave camp," said one.

"Where would you like to go if you were set free?" asked the other.

Almost in unison we replied, "To the U.S.A."

Soon after the visit was over we were called down to the reception room where, wonder of wonders, our measurements were taken and we were asked what color of suit we preferred, and what style of shoes and hat.

Two weeks passed, and we were impatient. The fitting had been completed and we were eager to go. Finally, wearing our prison clothes and with our new outfits in small suitcases, we were taken to a camp in Potma, some three hundred miles to the southeast in the Mordvinian Republic. Potma (Camp 5110-34) had held many Czarist prisoners at one time.

We were marched to an old, relatively small camp. Our suitcases were taken into security, we were checked in and, surprisingly, told to report for work at 8:00 A.M.

Three army cots were assigned to us in a half-empty room facing the gate. Within minutes the room was crowded. Dozens of questions were put to us: where from, what camp, when arrested, destination. The question as to our next destination interested us most. "Where *can* you go from here?" I asked.

Potma, they explained, was the repatriation camp. Sooner or later we should be going home. No one works here, they said, except for camp upkeep. This was at variance with what we were told at the gate. Was someone fooling us?

The next morning we did not report to work. A guard soon came and hauled us off to the camp commander, Lieutenant Litwinenko. He dressed us down for not obeying orders. I explained to him, on behalf of the three of

168

us, that we had been told in Moscow we were not going to another slave camp. If they wanted us to work they would have to send us back to a work camp. I told him that possibly most of the Yugoslavs, Austrians, Germans, Greeks, Spaniards, and Hungarians in this camp had fought against Russia at one time or another. But we Americans had done all we could to help Russia win the war. Without our help, I said, getting warmed up, Russia would have been wiped off the map. Now the camp administration wanted us to serve as examples so that they could force all those men to work for them.

Litwinenko's face was red with anger. Where had I learned Russian? he wanted to know.

"I learned it in your own camps," I said. He shook his head and mumbled that I could talk better than a Russian lawyer.

We did no work at Potma, except for light chores. With the help of European Red Cross packages, my ninety-five-pound frame took on thirty more pounds. They must be fattening me up for something, I thought—almost hopefully. But when months had passed and nothing had happened, I nearly lost hope.

I managed to send a postcard to an aunt in Berlin. Wonder of wonders, an answer came some weeks later. God must have intended that I receive this reply, for the guards were doing all in their power to keep me incommunicado. The censor, Major Baron, was on vacation, and the girl who had taken over promised to let me read any mail that might come, but she would have to take it back. Unfortunately, Baron returned on the day of mail delivery and was ready to take over. The girl merely picked up the cards that had come from the postoffice and, without having censored them, handed them to Baron in the camp,

169

among the men. Baron read out the names on the cards.

He read my name, and had I been right before him he would have remembered not to give the card to me; but someone quicker than his mental process grabbed for it, passing it on to me. It was the first line I had received, the first sign of life from the free world. It was September 26, 1954, more than nine and a quarter years since I had seen my mother. She and my father, thank God, were at home in Detroit. The card did not, of course, let me know what they were doing. I could not know at that time that the Soviets had stolen our home in Dresden, our clothing, our furniture, and our camera factories. The cameras (Praktiflex, Practica, and others) were sold and still are being sold in almost every American camera store. The profits go to the Communist Party. It was not enough that they should hold my father for seven years, or that I was still in their hands. They were doing everything to ruin us, even in the free world, by misusing trade marks and patents and by spreading false statements.

One thing the card did tell me, and that was that I was not alone in the world.

I was told that from that day I was a different human being. Now, more than ever, I protested, wrote petitions, demanded my rights. No fewer than twenty-five petitions were yet to be answered by the Soviets, but I was determined to rock their nerves.

The weeks in Potma again were moving slowly. New prisoners arrived every day. Periodically, men and women left for their homeland and freedom. A few days before I was to depart, an elderly woman arrived who was very much in the eyes of the guards. She was "Madame Gorskaja," the first wife of the new Soviet boss, Nikita

170

Khrushchev. She said virtually nothing about him or about their life together.

At last, on the evening of December 30, I was told that I was going back to Moscow on January 2, 1955. True to their word, I left Potma, arriving in Moscow on the third, the subject of what seemed VIP treatment at the hands of the Soviets. My new civilian woolen suit was given to me, and with Marchuk I was barracked in a fine home in the Bukova suburb of Moscow. I slept on the first real bed— a hard but real, individual bed—in more than nine years.

That afternoon a special delegation from the Kremlin itself came to see us. I jumped when I saw it was headed by General Masslennikov, the butcher of Vorkuta! He was accompanied by four colonels.

"You will leave for Berlin tomorrow, Mr. Noble, where you will be turned over to American authorities," Masslennikov said. "Meanwhile you will be shown Moscow by one of our officers."

I was really going home! And of all the irony, I was hearing it from Masslennikov! I was deliriously happy, but I controlled myself in front of the Russians.

Masslennikov shook my hand, then asked casually: "By the way, where were you in the Soviet Union?"

When I said "Vorkuta," the color drained from his face. "In which mine?" he asked, trying to maintain composure. "Mines 16 and 29," I answered. I was enjoying the game.

He squinted at me nervously, then asked: "Do you recognize me?"

"No," I lied, cautiously.

"Did you take part in the strike?"

"Certainly," I answered proudly. "We all did."

I spent the rest of the day seeing Moscow. I was not particularly impressed. Some of the main streets looked a little like those of western cities, but to go a hundred feet off a main thoroughfare was to take a trip back to the eighteenth century. The same people who had abused me for nine and a half years were now treating me as if I were a visiting schoolteacher on a summer vacation.

The next day, Marchuk and I, chaperoned by an MVD colonel, boarded the famous Blue Express from Moscow to East Berlin. Along the way, I thought how differently I was making the trip this time. In 1950 I had covered the same route on my stomach in a stinking Stalopinski. Now I was having a 35-ruble dinner on white tablecloths in the dining car, by courtesy of the MVD.

I was amazed at my own calmness as we rolled through Soviet and Polish territory. Every now and then a new set of officers would check our papers. "Where's the third man?" they would often ask. They were asking about Verdine, no doubt.

"I signed for him," the colonel would answer.

I couldn't imagine why they kept Verdine in Potma. The Soviets knew we would report his whereabouts as soon as we were free. Or were we not to be free?

American officers would meet us at the train, we were told. But we had learned that the more rank the Soviet officers display on their shoulder boards the less they tell the truth. The colonel accompanying us kept pointing out factories along the line and telling us the fine things that were made there: no arms, no tanks, nothing but the good things of life. As an example of what the factories were making, he called my attention to the charming little lamp on the table before the train window. I, in turn, pointed to a cast mark on the lamp which said "Made in Germany," and asked him if he might be mistaken. A cold smile and a change of subject was his reply.

Crossing the German border was an interesting experience. The train was examined from top to bottom. Every slit was checked. A spy might send a communication from Moscow to Berlin in a wall crack.

Later I was to learn why I was returning home in such fine style. Word brought to the U.S. by Homer Cox showed the door, and the postcard I had mailed over Rohrig's name from Vorkuta was the key. As soon as this reached my parents in Detroit, my father brought it directly to the State Department. The State Department dispatched another note to the Kremlin—from 1945 to the summer of 1954 the Russians had answered all U.S. notes with the statement that they had no knowledge of me. After the evidence was in the hands of our State Department, one note was sent after another, but the Soviets ignored them. Not one of these notes was acknowledged.

Meanwhile Congressman Alvin Bentley of Michigan had become interested in my case. He discussed it with President Eisenhower personally. In December 1954 the President sent a diplomatic note to Ambassador Bohlen in Moscow stating that our government had proof that I was a prisoner in the Soviet. Mr. Bohlen took it up directly with the Kremlin and soon I was on my way home.

The Blue Express brought me into East Berlin at 2:50 P.M. on January 8, 1955. No American officers were there to meet us. Fifteen minutes later I was in a room in Karlshorst, Soviet East Berlin HQ. There, I almost lost control of myself when a U.S. army liaison officer and two State Department officials walked in. One of the officials, Mr. Pratt, the U.S. consul in Berlin, signed a receipt for me. I must confess that, even though I had gone through nine

173

and a half years of degradation, starvation, Arctic cold, and the hardest of physical labor, I broke down at this moment. My resistance gave way and I cried with joy.

I was in the hands of the American authorities. Outside, I walked down the steps and into a State Department car that drove me to West Berlin and freedom. I had crossed a border that separated two worlds. The world of fear, terror, deceit, Godlessness, and slavery was behind me in the east. I was returning to the west, to a world of busy people developing their lives according to their abilities, a world of freedom and of moral standards almost unknown to the people of the Communist realm. From the Soviet Union, truly the richest country in respect to natural resources, but the poorest nation, I had come to a world of plenty which too often was not appreciated, for which too often gratitude was not expressed to God.

"Well, how does it feel to be back?" Mr. Pratt asked me.

I thought of Vorkuta, then looked out the window at the passing spectacle of the Western world. It was as if I had spent nine and a half years on some fierce, distorted satellite of the earth.

"Thank God," I answered. "I have so much to tell, I could not express it in words alone, Mr. Pratt."

At 1:30 A.M., the morning of January 17, 1955, I landed at Idlewild Airport, where I saw my family again.

I had been a slave in Russia; now I was free!

APPENDIX

APPENDIX

The following Soviet account provides an example of the manner in which the Communists fabricate and distort facts with which to feed their propaganda machine. Their purpose is to develop, in the Communist world, a greater apathy toward the West, and to convince the free world that the Soviets have good reason to violate international law and the basic rules of human behavior.

YESTERDAY THE NOBLES—
TODAY GENERAL GEHLEN*

by MAX SEYDEWITZ

        WEST BERLIN newspapers are publishing slanderous reports by American John Noble without, however, referring with one word to the criminal role which he and his father played as imperialist agents in Dresden during the Nazi war. The past of the Nobles and their activities in Germany are illuminated by Volkskammer Representative Max Seydewitz' book *The Destruction and Reconstruction of Dresden*. Following is an excerpted chapter from the book which is to be published shortly by the Kongress Verlag:

"The connections between American and German monopoly capitalists which never ceased during the war were intensified considerably toward the end of the war when the defeat of Hitlerite

* Translation from *Taegliche Rundschau* (Soviet occupation daily), January 13, 1955.

177

Germany and the failure of its world domination plans were inevitable. The efforts toward the establishment of a joint front against the Soviet Union, which had to be abandoned at the beginning of World War II because of the German imperialists' aggressive attempt at attaining world dominance, once again moved to the fore.

"The more the Soviet army cut the Fascist Wehrmacht to pieces and the more evident the total military defeat of Germany became, the more inclined were the defeated German imperialists to accept the offers of the imperialist American billionaires. This showed, during the last weeks of the war, also in the attitude of the Nazi leaders who were seeking opportunities to offer their services to the American imperialists. The secret collaboration of German and foreign destroyers of Germany which was gaining impetus toward the end of the war had many severe consequences for the German people, one being the destruction of the beautiful city of Dresden.

"In the final phase of the war, many of the important British and American agents, who were staying in Germany by order of their bosses, revealed their identity to the Nazi leaders. Many a Dresden resident will have wondered why the beautiful, large villa San Remo in the White Deer district, located in the immediate vicinity of the Loisenhof, was occupied by an American citizen by the name of Noble and his family who lived like millionaires and on whom no Nazi authority imposed any restrictions, save internment, as was the usage in times of war. Noble, let us presume, had been recommended by the gentlemen of the Standard Oil Company or General Motors to their business partners of the IG Farben as a particularly important person. Noble, it was indicated, was to organize, in the now declining war, the close cooperation of the German and American monopolists. So this American was persona grata also to the Nazi authorities. Noble's duties naturally included intrigues and espionages against the Soviet Union, and the gravediggers of Germany assisted him all too willingly. This, however, did not keep Noble from also spying on the Third Reich. For information on the Soviet Union which he received by wire from agents of his bosses in Wall Street and which he passed to the Nazi leaders, he obtained in return confidential information on Germany which he transmitted to his managers by wireless from villa San Remo.

"Thanks to the good work performed by Nazi-informed Mr. Noble, the Anglo-American headquarters had the best knowledge of conditions prevailing in Dresden. British Air Marshal Harris and General Spaatz, commander-in-chief of USAAF, knew exactly that Dresden was jammed with refugees and wounded. They knew the exact location of the densely populated residential quarters, of the 'Zwinger,' the 'Frauenkirche' and other cultural monuments and churches. They also knew where Dresden's military targets lay on which no bombs were dropped on February 13. They explicitly forbade the fliers to drop bombs on the White Deer district, for the Anglo-American headquarters by no means wished to endanger the life of its precious agent living in this area. For this reason, the White Deer was one of the few districts which were spared in the February 13 and 14 air raids.

"Although the Nazi leaders knew that the terror raid on Dresden had been directed by Mr. Noble, they refrained from arresting and punishing the American after the monstrous crime committed against the art city of Dresden and its population. The reasons therefor we find in a telephone conversation which Goebbels conducted at 4 A.M. on February 14 with Mutschmann who was sitting in a safe place at Grillenburg. In their conversation on the effects of the bomb raid on Dresden, which was taken down in shorthand and a stenographic report on which was available at the end of the war, Goebbels instructed the Saxon Gau leader 'not to lose contact with Noble,' for 'the man cannot be weighed up in gold.'

"Thereby Goebbels referred to the assistance which Noble had promised to the Nazi leaders for the time after the surrender. We can imagine what Noble and Mutschmann discussed during their secret meetings. The agent of the American billionaires certainly told the bankrupt Nazi Gau leader bluntly that the Nazis had lost their war and could save their future position only by surrendering to the men in Wall Street and by unconditionally recognizing the world-wide supremacy of the U.S.A. However, they would have to prove their readiness by immediate action, including their availability for the fight against the Soviet Union and their assistance in damming the growing influence of the Soviet Union before the war came to an end.

"Mutschmann, of course, was as willing as Goebbels and the other Nazi leaders on whose behalf he maintained contact with

Noble. That was why Mutschmann conscientiously carried out the instructions he had received from Goebbels. The Mutschmanns, Goebbelses and their like wanted to destroy, together with the Nobles and the men who had given orders for the destruction of Dresden, as much as possible of that part of Germany which had been laid down at the Yalta conference as the future Soviet Zone of occupation. The terrible sufferings and the tremendous damage thus inflicted upon the German people made no difference to the destroyers of Germany. What they wanted was licking the spittle of the American imperialists in order to save themselves from the disaster they had caused.

"The Nobles remained in their nice villa San Remo for some time after the war. They were instructed to continue the spying against the Soviet Union, which Noble had carried out already during the war, in the postwar Soviet occupation zone. But as Mutschmann, who while being Gau leader used to act the strong man and brutal dictator, turned out, after his arrest, to be a pitiable coward and weakling, he probably betrayed all about his collaboration with the Nobles and their activities.

"At any rate, the Nobles were stopped very early from continuing their criminal assignment. The beautiful villa San Remo first became the city guest house of Dresden and later was converted into a club house for the workers. From the terrace of the villa located on White Deer Hill the whole city can be overlooked. Surely, the Nobles were waiting in the night of that Tuesday for the punctual appearance of the 'Christmas trees' [popular German term for flares dropped by aircraft during night raids] over the dark silhouette of Dresden to show the bombers their target. Surely, the Nobles then stood at the window of villa San Remo, enjoying the macabre sight of the burning flames and of the collapsing precious cultural monuments and noting with heinous satisfaction the destruction of the art city of Dresden as well as the fulfillment of the mission which they directed and which the Nazi leaders supported.

"The destruction of the art city of Dresden shortly before the end of the war is only one example of the crimes which the secretly collaborating German imperialists, militarists, and Fascists and the Anglo-American imperialists committed against the German people. Since the end of World War II, the German and foreign destroyers of Germany have been collaborating openly for quite a while, and their objective is the preparation of another imperialist smash-and-grab war and of further horrible crimes against the peoples.

"In order to prepare the war which the American imperialists want to wage for the conquest of the world, a number of proposals were laid down in the official American report on the results of the Anglo-American air war against Germany, the 'United States Strategic Bombing Survey.' From the fact that the whole air war did not suffice to decrease German armament production, that the terror raids on German cities in which the houses of the civilian population were destroyed and women and children were murdered were without military significance, the official American document failed to draw the consequence, namely, to renounce this kind of air warfare and prohibit mass extermination media in future wars. On the contrary, it was proposed to intensify the strategic air warfare in the next war and 'to select the targets of air raids more carefully' than during World War II. That is, not to attack all possible armament enterprises with insufficient means but to concentrate the raids on centers of gravity mentioned in the reports as 'gasoline, chemicals, steel, electricity and the traffic net.' In order to always be able to raid these centers uninterruptedly with a superior air force, the document's authors recommended to the U.S. rulers the expansion of a powerful U.S. air force because, in their opinion, the air force will play a great role in the next war in the 'connection of atom bomb and remote-controlled missiles with trans-oceanic range.' Because—the official American document continues—there would be 'no greater mistake than assuming that the practices and policies which led to victory during the Second World War will be sufficient for the next one.'

"The improved practices recommended here which had already been used to prepare the war and which had been applied in the cold war include espionage and sabotage activities employed by the United States in Germany and all countries of the peace camp. The 'United States Strategic Bombing Survey' stated that it was difficult in the beginning of the air war against Germany to recognize the targets, since the United States, at that time, did not have a working espionage organization in Germany and the Air Force command lacked data on important targets. The official

181

American report says literally: 'There was no cooperation between military and other organizations—regardless of their private or official character. It developed only during the war. Experience has taught that it is better that such institutions exist all the time' [that is, also in peace time.—Author].

"In line with this proposal the American imperialists continued to maintain and even enlarge their espionage organization established in Germany after the end of the war in order to create an instrument for the next war prepared by them. The basis for the expansion of the American espionage net was laid already during the last months of World War II in cooperation with the Nobles and Mutschmanns.

"This cooperation resulted in the transfer of the Nazi espionage apparatus into American services. The German Nazis who raved most loudly against the American plutocrats during the Nazi regime have been working, since the end of the war, for the realization of the world conquest plans of the American imperialists. Among those working currently for the American espionage center are numerous Nazi war criminals sentenced by courts but freed from prisons by the Americans. Nazi General Gehlen is heading the thus reinforced Fascist espionage organization, whose leading members are former SS and Gestapo leaders. The Gehlen organization's activities are an example of the American imperialists' and German Fascists' open collaboration in the preparation of another war.

"The criminal tactics of the U.S. imperialism-serving Gehlen espionage organization, exercised illegally in the German Democratic Republic against the vital interests of all German people, were revealed by numerous of its members who did not want to continue participating in this crime. This fact was stressed in all proceedings of the German Democratic Republic's Supreme Court against Gehlen agents. Early in November 1954, for instance, main defendant Bandelow in the process against the Bandelow gang admitted that he had been committed to act according to the 'General Order for All' which was found in his possession. This order contained minutely detailed instructions for the case of war. Every agent received detailed instructions about his duties in case of the repeated dropping of American bombs on German soil. By means of radio equipment found on them and with the aid of other facilities, the Gehlen spies were to report the results of the terror raids on traffic facilities, railroads, bridges, streets, power plants, etc., and keep their employers continuously informed on important targets, as well as newly constructed railroads, bridges and streets."

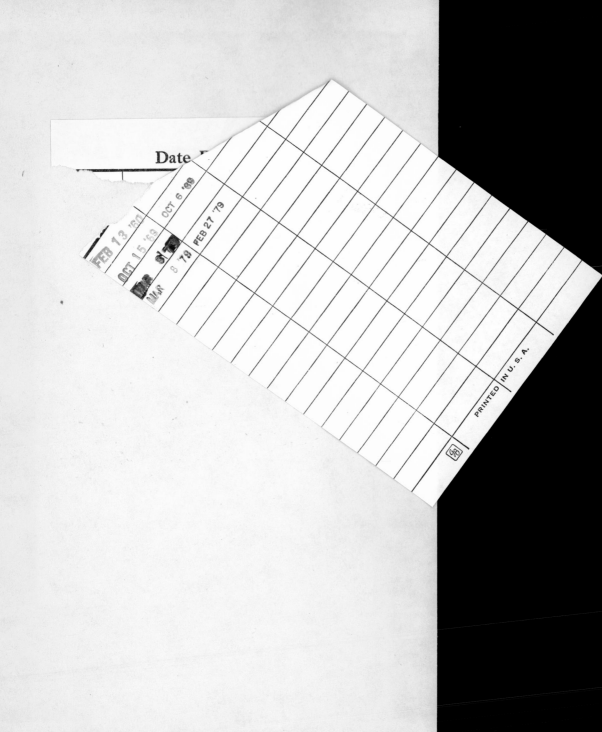

Date

FEB 13 '60

OCT 15 '69   OCT 6 '69

MAR   8 '79   FEB 27 '79

PRINTED IN U. S. A.